# GENERAL GEORGE HANNIBAL BUSCH
# AND THE SEARCH FOR THE
# LITTLE BIG OIL WELL


By
DAVID L. CHISLING


Illustrations drawn by
ALEXANDRIA NABINGER

Illustration notes created and written by
AUTHOR

I

This cartoon storybook is dedicated to the members of
Monty Python, living and deceased, whom without the
Training I received in their infamous and feared "Flying Circus",
I would not have had the proper military experience and
Knowledge to write this sordid tale of
War, politics, big business, and religion!

**Cry havoc-and let slip the dogs of war!**

SHAKESPEARE/RICHARD III – 1590

Order this book online at www.trafford.com
or email orders@trafford.com

Most Trafford titles are also available at major online book retailers.

© Copyright 2011 David L. Chisling
All rights reserved. No part of this publication may be reproduced, stored in a retrieval system, or
transmitted, in any form or by any means, electronic, mechanical, photocopying, recording, or
otherwise, without the written prior permission of the author.

Note for Librarians: A cataloguing record for this book is available from Library
and Archives Canada at www.collectionscanada.ca/amicus/index-e.html

Printed in the United States of America.

ISBN: 978-1-4251-7136-0 (sc)
ISBN: 978-1-4251-8086-7 (e)

Trafford rev. 11/11/2011

www.trafford.com

North America & international
toll-free: 1 888 232 4444 (USA & Canada)
phone: 250 383 6864 ♦ fax: 812 355 4082

## PREFACE

### And now for something completely different...

    This cartoon storybook is merely a satirical interpretation of political, military, and economic events of the early 22nd Century.  Please!  Do not take this cartoon storybook too seriously.  Protesting and rioting over these illustrations is strictly forbidden by the United Nations Human Rights Humor Commission.  Please respect the rights of political satirists!

    Official names of politicians and military leaders have been deleted or changed, in order to confuse and offend conservative political extremists and religious fanatics even more!  Except of course, the deceased generals of history such as Hannibal, George Armstrong Custer, and countless Field-Marshals of the Imperial German Army, whom I do not think will be offended by this, since they are all dead!  In fact, I believe they would be flattered that the main character in this heroic and humorous tale of war is a model of their military prowess and dress.

    A special tribute for this book must be made to General George Armstrong Custer.  Custer's disastrous campaign against hostile Indian forces in 1876, that led him into the Little Big Horn to be massacred in an epic last stand with his 7th Calvary, triggered and intriguing idea in my mind during the heated U.S. Presidential election of 2004.  This simple idea was the inspiration for a satirical comparison of the 19th Century military disaster, with a potential 21st Century military disaster for the United States of America.

    Hence, I now give you the tale of General George Hannibal Busch and the epic Battle of the Little Big Oil Well in the great U.S.-Iraq Wars of the 22nd Century.

THE AUTHOR-2007

# CONTENTS

## GENERAL GEORGE HANNIBAL BUSH AND THE SEARCH FOR THE LITTLE BIG OIL WELL

It is men who endure toil and dare, and danger, that achieve glorious deeds, and it is a lovely thing to live with courage, and to die leaving behind an everlasting renown.

RICHARD BURTON AS ALEXANDER THE GREAT (MGM-1955)


There has never been a just one, never an honorable one-on the part of the instigator of the war. I can see a million years ahead, and the rule will never change in so many as half a dozen instances. The loud little handful-as usual-will shout for the war. The pulpit will-warily and cautiously-object-at first; the great, big dull bulk of the nation will rub its sleepy eyes and try to make out why there should be a war, and will say, earnestly and indignantly-it is unjust and dishonorable, and there is no necessity for it-then the handful will shout louder.

MARK TWAIN – 1900


Let us be thankful for the fools. But for them the rest of us could not succeed.

Mark Twain - 1897


The die is cast.

JULIUS CAESAR – 49 B.C.

**THE LITERARY BUCCANEER!**
"The Scourge of the Establishment Main!"

**Illustrated by Orest Hyrcyk**

David L. Chisling was born on 24 February 1957, the son of an American military career father and European mother. Required to earn a living after high school, he became an eccentric University Bohemian of Classic History studies, specializing in Military History. Before and after finishing college, he led a wandering adventurous life as a swashbuckler of the U.S. Navy and Merchant Marine, earning the nickname-Navy Davey. Before the catastrophic years of the early 21$^{st}$ Century's War on Terror, David wrote a four-volume satire about university life. Five years after the American 9/11, he began writing this Gargantuan Book, whose purpose was to inflame the world to question the powers that be, through the virility of its satire. According to the original plan, this book would expand up to a six-volume satire of the War on Terror. Branded as extremely politically incorrect by the Neo-Conservative political and religious factions of America, this Europeanized-American writer's future remains a dark mystery!?

**Dead men tell no tales.**
ENGLISH PIRATES-17TH CENTURY

**Here's-Navy Davey!**
SGT. CURLY BUSCH-2106

NEW YORK
2006

VII

## SECTION I: FIRST IRAQ WAR AND INTER-WAR CARTOONS

## THE TOP SECRET PLAN!

General George Hannibal Busch discusses brilliant strategy in the White House War Room with the Vice President and Secretary of Defense, prior to Operation Enduring Oil Supply in January of 2103.

**War is a continuation of state policy-by other means.**

KARL VON CLAUSEWITZ-1818

## WILD STUDENT!

George Hannibal Busch came from a very wealthy and powerful family of Confederate Texan oil magnates, who had their roots as D@#*&$ Yankees from New England?? George's father became extremely successful in national politics, and would one day become President of the United States of America. When George became of age by graduating high school with a G.E.D., and no recorded S.A.T.s or A.C.T.s, his father bribed Ivy League Officials to enroll his son at a leading university. Once at the school, George joined a peaceful, charitable fraternity that promoted universal brotherhood. George managed to maintain a gentlemanly C grade average, as he occupied his valuable study time with fraternity charitable events. George Hannibal's favorite form of recreation would foreshadow his future fame, which was to play the game of Risk with fellow students and kick their a#$#@!, even if cheating were involved. Upon graduating with little job prospects due to his low grade G.P.A., and lack of contacts due to school unpopularity, George Hannibal's father shipped him off to U.S. Army Officer Candidate School. George Hannibal graduated first in his class at this school, and was commissioned a 2nd Lieutenant. George Hannibal volunteered for the U.S. Cavalry, and dreamed of someday leading the tanks on his privately owned Republican elephant. The rest is now history...................

**My brother George's behavior in college made the movie "Animal House" look like a Sunday morning T.V. religious show and prayer meeting by comparison.**

SGT. CURLY BUSCH-2111

## CAMPAIGN MAP OF OPERATION STORM THE DESERT OIL FIELDS-2091

General Busch's misdirected and misguided infamous advance is highlighted in this campaign map of the first Iraq War. This heroic and bold march of confusion would later earn him the Medal of Dubious Distinction, presented to him by his President Daddy of the United States.

**When the U.S. Cavalry is lost in the desert, what kind of map do they use to find their way out back to the fort?**

**Sandpaper!**

OLD AMERICAN INDIAN JOKE-19TH CENTURY

6

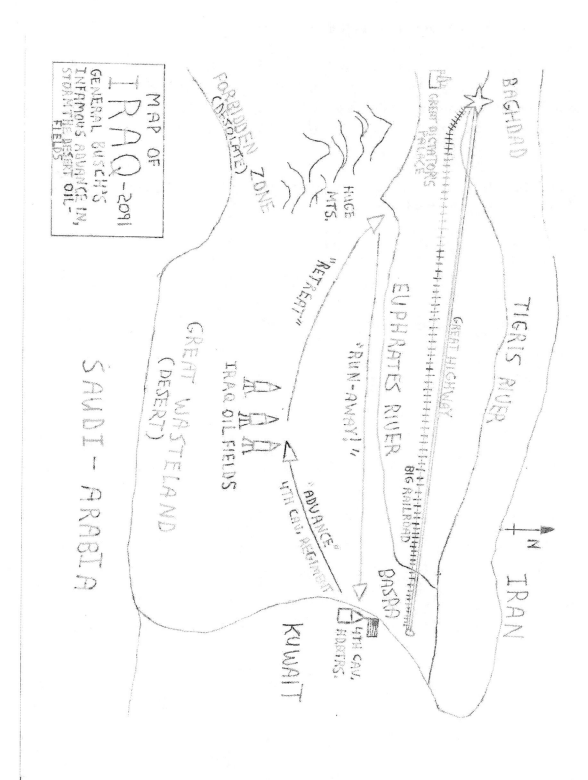

## RETREAT!

General George Busch conducted an infamous campaign across the Iraq Desert, to capture the country's profitable oil fields in Operation Storm the Desert Oil Fields, which ended in a humiliating defeat! George marched the 4th Cavalry Regiment to the oil fields and was preparing to capture them, when he encountered the Great Dictator of Iraq's elite force of Republican Guards that had been sent to defend the installations. General Busch canceled his attack, when the Republican Guard General Crazy Camel (whom George would trick and humiliate in the next Iraq War), threatened to confiscate George's Republican Party registration card if he dared to attack fellow Republicans. Crazy Camel's ruse worked, as a naive General Busch ordered a retreat of his regiment towards Baghdad, and this misguided direction of travel caused a subsequent flight of panic back to 4th Cavalry Headquarters. This operational fiasco caused bewildered anger at Field Marshal Storm'n Von Norton's headquarters. George's superior officer sent a communiqué to the President at the White House, to complain about his son's cowardly performance. General Busch's Daddy President, however, conveniently hushed-up the matter and decided to redeem his son's honor by sending him on a Top Secret Mission?

**One should never run away from a silly fight.**

SGT. CURLY BUSCH-2108

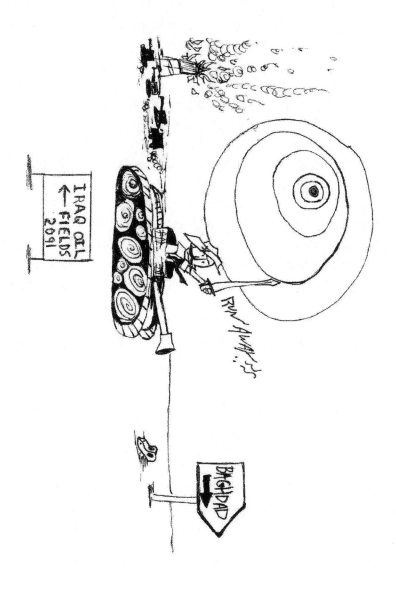

## CAPTURED!

Brigadier General George Busch is sent on a top secret mission by his Daddy President to capture the Great Dictator of Iraq. White House intelligence sources with the C.I.A. confirm that the Great Dictator is trying to escape his defeated country by sneaking over the Syrian border to seek asylum with Syria's Smaller Dictator. George through sheer luck, after days of wandering the border, accidentally stumbles upon the Great Dictator who is dressed in fancy attire, and arrests the tyrant in the name of his Daddy President. The top secret mission was a complete success!

**When one is running away from something, he'd better d#$@& well know where he's going to hide away!**

SGT. CURLY BUSCH-2108

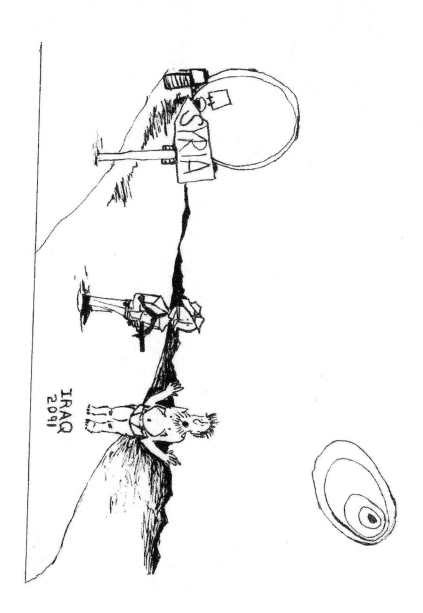

## BRAVEHEART!

Upon capturing the Great Dictator of Iraq, Brigadier General George Busch was promoted to Major General by his Daddy President. The President also proclaimed his son George to be a national hero for his exceptional bravery and actions during Operation Storm the Desert Oil Fields. When the President visited Kuwait to celebrate the U.S. Victory over Iraq, he awarded the Medal of Dubious Distinction to his son in a special ceremony attended by the Army Commander of the Iraq War, Field Marshal Von Storm'n Norton. Norton salutes with solemn respect as the captured Great Dictator expresses his opinion with a world-wide gesture of respect.

**Like the great Scottish hero of the 13ᵗʰ Century who was never loyal to the English King Edward I, I never truly believed that my brother George was completely loyal to our Daddy President. William Wallace stated he was not a traitor, because he never swore loyalty to Edward in the first place. Likewise, my brother told me once that he could never be a complete traitor to Daddy; he simply could not read the loyalty statement he was supposed to recite to our Daddy President.**

SGT. CURLY BUSCH-2108

## FRESH MEAT!

The finest youth of America who have enlisted in the U.S. Army, will volunteer for service in Major General Busch's 4$^{th}$ Cavalry Regiment. The regiment's headquarters are located at Fort Custer in Little Big Horn, Montana. It was ironic that this gruesome location from American Military History would be a prelude to the entertaining and misguided Battle of the Little Big Oil Well in the upcoming second Iraq War.

**The Army does not want to train robots.  It wants to produce killers!**

SGT. CURLY BUSCH-2108

## NEW TORY ALLY!

During the inter-war years, General George Busch embarks overseas on a secret mission for the neo-conservative vice president, in order to recruit new allies for the upcoming second Iraq War. The Prime Minister of Great Britain, named Tony Baloney, gives George a message for his boss-that Britain will gladly support the next Iraq invasion, provided they will share in the oil profits.

**God bless the Limey Baloney!**

SGT. CURLY BUSCH-2108

## ACT OF WAR!

The great terrorist attack by Third World Criminals on the oil installation that provides precious discount-priced gas to the politicians, bureaucrats, and lobbyists of the nation's capital. Neo-conservative war hawks, led by the vice president, quickly accused and produced silly evidence that the Great Dictator of Iraq was directly involved in the attack, with its master mind-The #1 Terrorist of the World. More silly evidence was produced by the war hawks, that the Great Dictator was hoarding Weapons of Mass Insignificance inside Iraq. The American Nation bought into it-war was imminent!

**This is a day that will live in mediocrity!**

SGT. CURLY BUSCH-2112

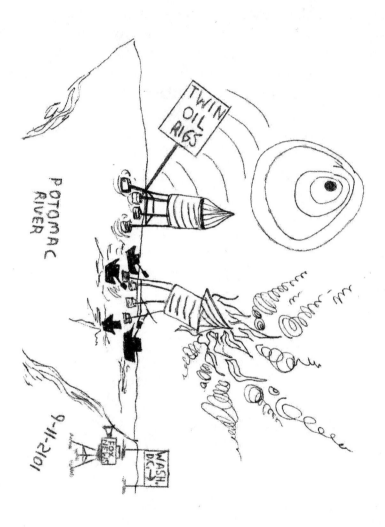

## GLADIATOR!

General George Hannibal Busch and the 4th Cavalry Regiment pay their respects to the Great Leader of America, before bravely embarking upon the dangerous mission to liberate a 3rd World Country from its dictator.  Thus will begin the United State's Global Crusade to rid the world of evil, and initiate the new-War of Horror!

**There have been many Gladiator movies made in Hollywood; maybe they will make one about my brother and I fighting in Iraq.  They might name it, "Running Away To Hide Somewhere In The Coliseum, And Buying Your Way Out With The Emperor".**

SGT. CURLY BUSCH-2109

## SIBLING RIVALRY!

General George Busch training his part Democrat and half brother, the underachieving Corporal Curly Busch, in the art of scouting for the 4th Cavalry Regiment. The training was conducted on the Kuwait/Iraq border, prior to the second Iraq War. Curly was the illegitimate child of their Daddy President's secret mistress, who was rumored to have been a sexy campaign fund-raiser for the Democratic Party. This caused quite an underground scandal with the Republican Daddy's wife, and members of the neo-conservative inner circle. But, Daddy survived the storm and emerged as a future U.S. President, who would breed two famous sons for America's future wars of conquest.

**When my father and his mistress bred me, they really broke the mildew!**

SGT. CURLY BUSCH-2110

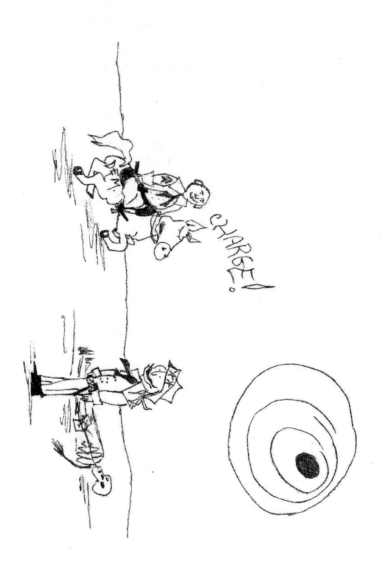

## ANGRY SECRETARY OF STATE!

The first Secretary of State, nicknamed the more humane one, challenges the Vice President and Secretary of Defense on the validity and accuracy of government intelligence information in launching the upcoming second Iraq War. The Secretary of State angrily emphasizes that the official story given for starting the war to the American people, concerning Iraq's link to the #1 Terrorist and Weapons of Little or No Significance, is not the whole truth behind Operation Enduring Oil Supply.

**I have seen the enemy, and it is we!**

SGT. CURLY BUSCH-2108

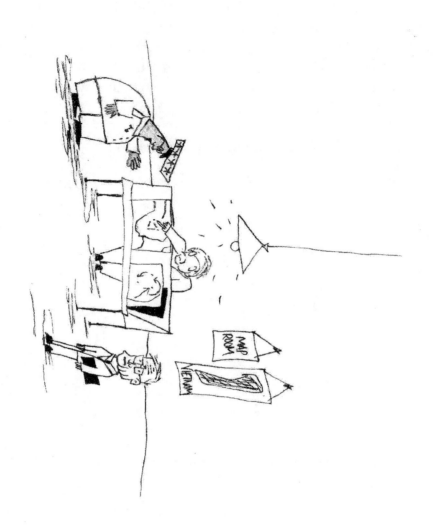

## BLESS THE TROOPS!

The holy and beloved #1 religious celebrity of America, the world famous Reverend Biggy Grand, visits Kuwait on the eve of the upcoming second Iraq War. He proudly and passionately gives divine inspiration and protection in a big grand speech to General Busch and his 4th Cavalry Regiment. The almighty Christian God observes the religious pep talk with grim satisfaction from Heaven.

**Napoleon was correct, God has nothing to do with war, for it is solely the domain of the Devil.**

SGT. CURLY BUSCH-2108

## SECTION II: SECOND INVASION OF IRAQ CARTOONS

### TALLY-HO!

General George Busch leads tanks of the 4th Cavalry Regiment across the Kuwait border into Iraq, to begin Operation Enduring Oil Supply on 20 March, 2103.  In front of him stood the formidable modern Iraq Army of the Great Dictator, prepared to defend their beloved nation and its vast precious oil fields.

**Veni, Vidi, Vici-I came, I saw, I conquered!**

JULIUS CAESAR-47 B.C.

## CAMPAIGN MAP OF OPERATION ENDURING OIL SUPPLY-2103

General Busch's confused and disorderly infamous advance is highlighted in this campaign map of the second Iraq War.  This heroic and bold unauthorized march of profit seeking towards the Little Big Oil Well, would later earn him the Medal of Oil, presented to him by the Secretary of Defense on behalf of the grateful Vice President of the United States.

**When your boss orders you to get somewhere, make sure you know exactly where you're going!**

SGT. CURLY BUSCH-2110

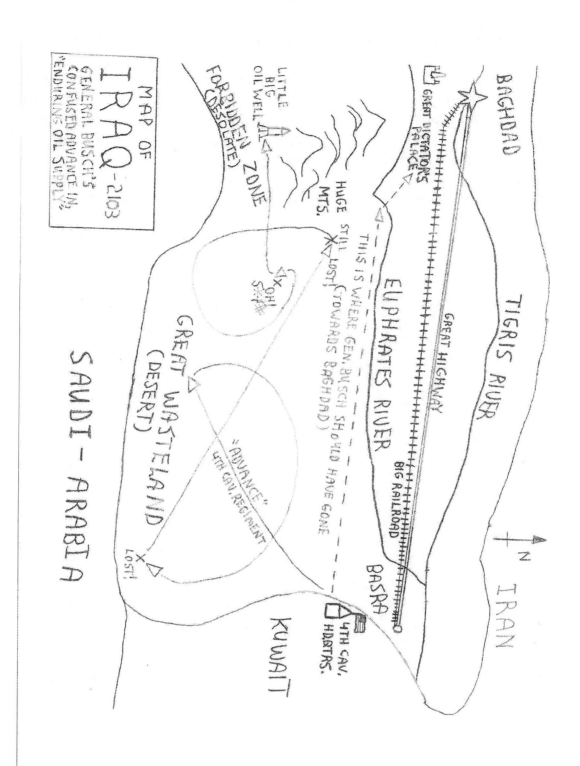

## BRIDGE TO THE FUTURE!

General George Busch leads his 4th Cavalry Regiment across the previous President's Peace Bridge, to conduct the gruesome assault upon Iraq in Operation Enduring Oil Supply.  The political goals of peace, prosperity, and stability for the world as dreamed of by the previous U.S. President, were now crushed into the dustbin of history by the tank treads of Bloody Busch for a Neo-Conservative government that promoted war, profit, and power!

**I get my troops there the fastest, farthest, with the mostest.**

GEN. NATHAN BEDFORD FORREST-1862

## BLITZKRIEG OVER BAGHDAD!

The commander of the U.S. Air Force in Operation Enduring Oil Supply is the Baron Von Busch, who is the cousin of General George Busch.  The Baron successfully completed his assigned mission of confidently bombing Baghdad into rubble.  An avid W.W.II History buff, the Baron led the air assault in his personally restored antique German Luftwaffe Stuka Dive Bomber.

**We'll bomb them back into the Stone Age!**

GEN. CURTIS LEMAY-1967

## LOST IN THE DESERT!

Corporal Curly Busch nervously tells his half brother General George Busch that he cannot locate the elusive Little Big Oil Well at this time. The 4th Cavalry had been originally ordered by high command to march towards Baghdad and assist other military units in capturing the capital city. However, George had other ideas as he secretly led his regiment across the wastelands of the Iraq Desert, towards the Forbidden Zone that concealed the top prize for capture in the war-the highly profitable Little Big Oil Well! The risky journey was plagued by constant confusion and anxiety due to being lost several times. Eventually through Curly's scouting skills and blind luck, the 4th Cavalry found their objective.

**Unlike Field Marshal Rommel of W.W.II fame, the 4th Cavalry marched through the desert like a demented fox that was so rabid for profit, it had lost all its sense of direction and military purpose.**

SGT. CURLY BUSCH-2111

## CUSTER'S GHOST!

General George Busch confronts the tortured spirit from Hell of General George Custer, one night on the march towards Little Big Oil Well. Custer warns Busch about the prophecy of doom in conducting foolish military adventures that lead to official and public condemnation. Busch assures Custer that unlike the disaster at the Little Big Horn, the march on the Little Big Oil Well will succeed because Mother Profit and the current Neo-Conservative Government are faithfully behind him.

**Better to rule the Little Big Oil Well, than serve as a government pauper.**

FIELD MARSHAL VON BUSCH-2105

## CURLY'S WARNING!

After long tribulations, Corporal Curly Busch finally locates and scouts the Little Big Oil Well.  He tells his half brother, the Neo-Conservative General George Hannibal Busch that the oil well is ironically defended by the strong and numerous formations of the notorious Iraq Republican Guards.  There is also a strong fortress positioned there called Fort Crazy Camel, named after the Iraq General in command.  George is not intimidated, and orders a general advance of the 4th Cavalry to do battle with his fellow Republicans.  George Busch now changed uniforms to match his middle name, and rode his personal Republican elephant into battle.  The elephant's nickname was Traveling Plunderer. Bloody Hannibal Busch now sought to emulate the famous Carthaginian conquering general of ancient history, who crossed the Alps with elephants to do battle with the Roman Empire.

**The only good Republican, is a dead Republican!**

SGT. CURLY BUSCH-2112

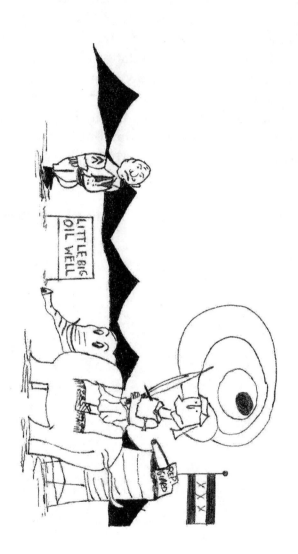

## DUEL IN THE SKY!

Baron Von Busch engages the Great Dictator and his formidable modern air force in a dog-fight in the skies over Iraq.  The U.S. Air Force objective was to gain complete air superiority for U.S. Military forces in their quest for victory in Operation Enduring Oil Supply.  Baron Von Busch's lightning attack on the Great Dictator's aircraft was so sudden and successful, it became known in the annals of U.S. Military History as-**30 Seconds Over The Little Big Oil Well!**

**Never was so little owed by so few,  to so many who simply  did not give a s#$%.**

SGT. CURLY BUSCH-2110

## BATTLE PLAN MAP FOR THE BATTLE OF THE LITTLE BIG OIL WELL-2103

This map shows General Hannibal Busch's brilliant plan to destroy the Iraq Republican Guard defenses, and capture the Little Big Oil Well. George's strategy was simple and direct, depending entirely on sheer courage and blind luck. No consideration was given to protect the 4th Cavalry Regiment's flanks, or locate and deal with any enemy reserve forces hidden for a counterattack. Perhaps Bloody Busch's confidence and intelligence were in question when he gave a foul gesture to his troops behind their backs as the battle commenced. Certainly his mental stability was long in doubt, when such a suicidal and inept battle plan was first devised by him.

**My brother's battle plan at the Little Big Oil Well was very good; he simply forgot to work out the details.**

SGT. CURLY BUSCH-2110

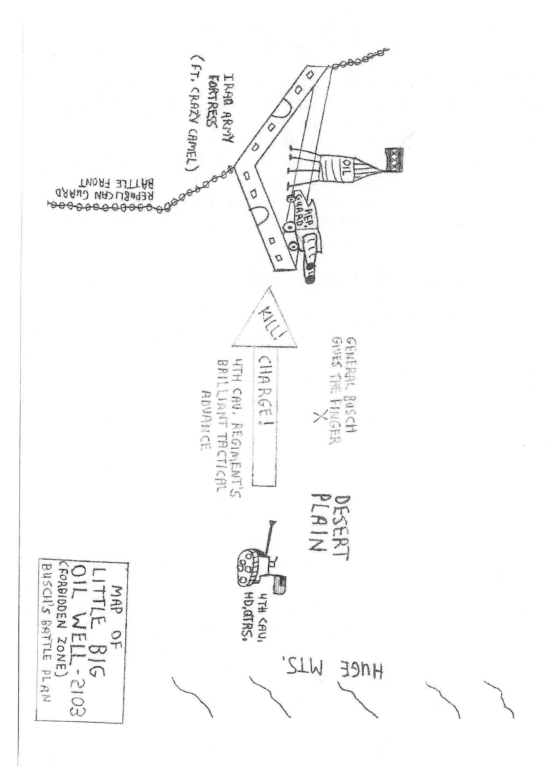

## BATTLE MAP FOR THE BATTLE OF THE LITTLE BIG OIL WELL-2103

This map shows the actual battle events of the fight to capture the fortress of the Little Big Oil Well. General Hannibal Busch's battle plan did not go exactly as planned. However, after a long silly and desperate fight, the oil well was captured and the Republican Guard cowards tricked into surrendering. Key events of the battle were the disastrous frontal assault, followed by panic and retreat, and culminating in desperate last stands against Iraq counterattacks. The day was saved when George single-handedly made a defiant last stand against Republican Guard General Crazy Camel. This rattled and unnerved the confused Crazy Camel so much he decided to surrender to his cunning fellow Republican Busch. The only smart soldier of the 4th Cavalry Regiment was Corporal Curly Busch, who fled the near disastrous battle rather than be killed or captured. He then had a ring-side seat from the mountains drinking cool beer, as he witnessed the battle's climax and American victory through his scout binoculars.

**No battle plan survives the first five minutes of an encounter with the enemy.**

HELMUTH KARL GRAF VON MOLTKE-1871

**Every battle plan changes at the firing of the first fart.**

SGT. CURLY BUSCH-2106

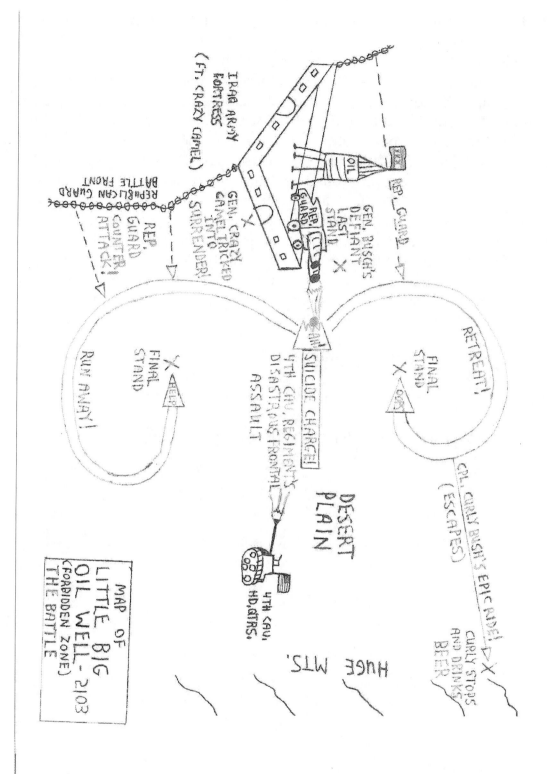

## THE FINGER!

The Neo-Conservative Hannibal Busch flips off his troopers of the 4<sup>th</sup> Cavalry behind their backs as they launch their suicidal attack against fellow beloved Republican Guards. The general desperately wanted to win the battle, but found it irritating to be fighting against other Republicans from another part of the world. It pained George's bloody heart that Global Republicans would ever fight each other so!

**Sometimes my serious power-hungry brother George can be goofier than me.**

SGT. CURLY BUSCH-2108

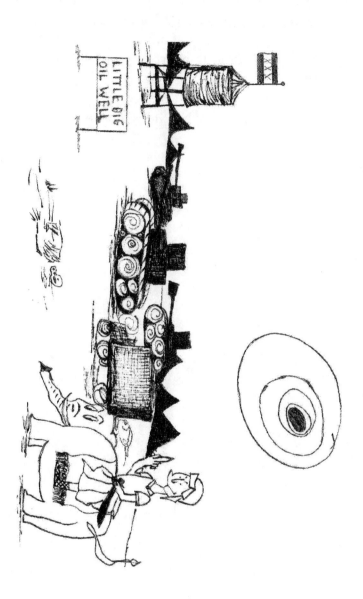

## NO RUNNING AWAY!

The Neo-Conservative General Hannibal Busch exhorts his troopers of the 4th Cavalry not to yield in the face of overwhelming numbers of fellow invincible Iraq Republican Guards. George orders that there will be no retreat! Any soldier caught retreating will be thrown out of the Republican Party. A handful of Democrats disobeyed and did run, including George's half brother and part Democrat Corporal Busch. Curly fled from the battlefield to scout the rear areas for enemy movement, and took a relaxing beer break to observe the rest of the battle through his binoculars.

**The army at Stalingrad, will fight to the last man, last bullet.**

ADOLF HITLER-1943

## DOOMED COMMAND!

The Neo-Conservative General Hannibal Busch faces off alone in defiant desperation against his fellow Republican Guards.  The rest of the 4th Cavalry had retreated in panic and were being assaulted by an enemy counterattack.  Even his brother Curly had deserted him and fled the battle for a beer break.  In one last act of amazing courage to turn the tide of battle, the heroic George confronted the enemy single-handedly, in order to intimidate and trick his fellow Republicans into doing what he does best-surrender as a noble coward.

**Merde! The Old Guard dies, but does not yield!**

MARSHAL PIERRE CHAMBRONNE-1815

52

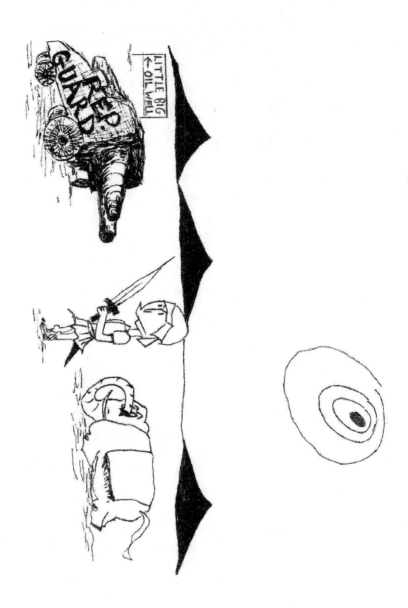

## NUTTY GENERAL!

The Commander of the Iraq Republican Guards at the Little Big Oil Well was General Crazy Camel. The Great Dictator of Iraq considered him to be one of his most trusted and finest generals. That is the reason why the Iraq leader entrusted Crazy Camel to defend his most prized and profitable installation in the whole country. The only weakness with Crazy Camel was that he suffered with mental instability. This was due to his constant exposure from the filthy stench of his unwashed desert soldiers in this scorching hot, isolated and barren position in the Forbidden Zone.

**He (Adolf Hitler) lives in the fantasy land of the cuckoo land!**

FIELD MARSHAL ROMMEL-1944

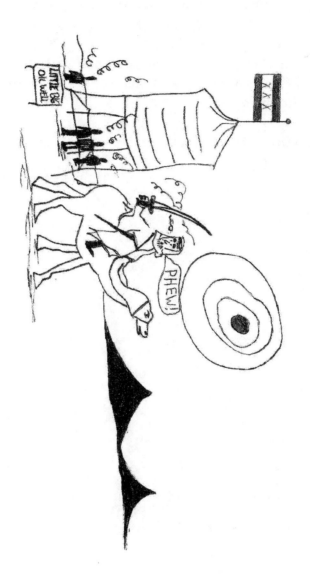

## TRAITOR TO THE GREAT DICTATOR!

General Hannibal Busch finally confronts the Republican Guard leader to face-to-face mortal combat. George reasons that he cannot defeat the whole enemy force; he must seek out and confront their leader in order to capture or kill him. This should cause the rest of the enemies to retreat or surrender. Bloody Busch's plan works perfectly, as he finally hunts down the mentally imbalanced General Crazy Camel and cunningly tricks him into surrendering himself and his entire command. General Busch had achieved another common event over his Republican Guard rival-which was a Neo-Conservative Republican who tricked an unwilling regular Republican into submitting to their extreme will!

**Never trust a traitor, even one you create.**

BARON HARKONNEN(DUNE BOOKS)-+20000 A.D.

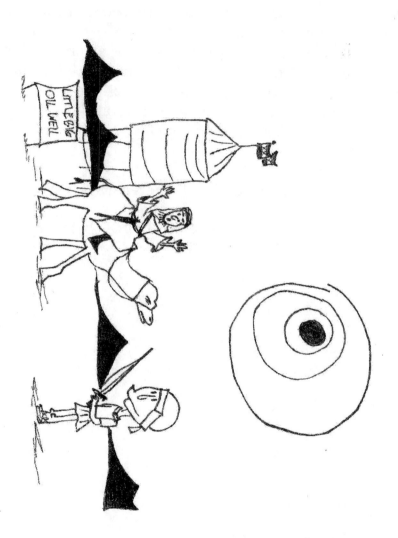

## BUSCH OF ARABIA!

Upon the surrender of General Crazy Camel and his command, General George Busch proudly raised the American Flag atop the Little Big Oil Well and notified U.S. High Command of his mysterious whereabouts and miraculous victory. The American media immediately swooped upon the site, and George cleverly staged a political publicity stunt in front of the cameras to enhance his image as the great military hero of the Iraq Wars. This immediate popularity over an amazing victory, gave him a promotion to Lieutenant General for his brave deeds.

**My brother's brave deeds will live forever in the anus of American Military History!**

SGT. CURLY BUSCH-2109

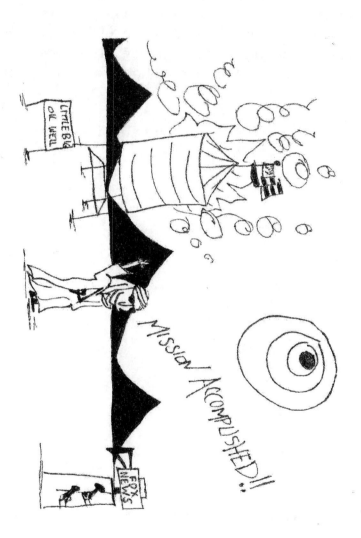

## OLD BLOOD AND OIL!

The swift advance and outstanding capture of the Little Big Oil Well by General George Hannibal Busch was soon compared to the famous exploits of General George Patton of W.W. II by the American Media and general public. However, not all the soldiers of the 4th Cavalry who were involved in the Iraq Campaign were so complimentary towards their leader. Thus began an infamous nickname given to Bloody Busch from his loyal and affectionate troops as George rode off into the sunset with his spoils of war.

**Unlike Patton with Rommel, my brother was not literate enough to read Patton's books.**

SGT. CURLY BUSCH-2110

## CLEVER EXCUSES!

The newly promoted Lieutenant General George Busch makes countless excuses to the U.S. Army High Command about why he cannot assist other army units in their bloody assault to capture Baghdad. Headquarters was already displeased that General Busch had disobeyed orders, and secretly marched to capture the Little Big Oil Well.  However, Bloody Busch's surprising victory had gained him too much support with the Vice President, media, and the American public for any action to be taken for his insubordination by headquarters. George now argues and tells the commander of all U.S. Forces in Iraq that he must and will keep his 4th Cavalry Regiment positioned at the profitable oil well, for security reasons.  George's boss, who is Field Marshal Von Toasted Beans Franks-Hamburger, is livid with rage and promises extreme action and punishment for General Busch if the 4th Cavalry does not march towards Iraq's Capital.

**Everyone makes countless excuses in their lifetime.  My brother only ever made one-money!**

SGT. CURLY BUSCH-2111

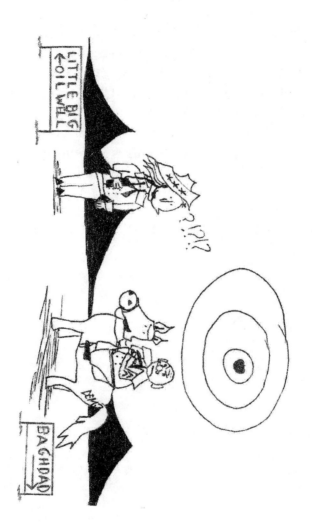

## BATTLE OF BAGHDAD BAY!

Illustrated by Jim Coon

With the conclusion of the epic battle of the Little Big Oil Well, the bigger and more decisive Battle for Baghdad began, which would end the war in a great U.S. Victory if captured. The overall commander of American forces in Iraq, the esteemed Field Marshal Von Toasty (short for Toasted Beans) Franks-Hamburger decided to initially use the vaunted U.S. Navy to capture the city in a surprise amphibious naval attack. The commander of this sneak attack would be the uncle of General George Busch, the renowned Admiral Dewey Busch. Accompanying the Admiral would be Seaman Curly Busch, whom General Busch had dispatched from the Little Big Oil Well to assist his uncle as the forward lookout and gunner on the old admiral's flag ship-The Golden Behind. The attack began early in the morning on the Tigris River outside of Baghdad. As The Golden Behind sailed in to bombard the capital city, the Great Dictator's powerful modern Navy suddenly appeared upstream to intercept the U.S. Fleet. Curly was so busy loading the forward cannon, he failed to spot the Great Dictator's Fleet until it was too late. As the two fleets closed distance to engage in mortal naval combat, Admiral Dewey Busch gave the order to fire! Seaman Busch pulled the cannon cord to blow the Great Dictator's flagship from the water, but nothing happened! In his panic at not spotting the enemy fleet sooner, Curly forgot to finish loading the cannon. The result was a misfire and subsequent rapid retreat as Admiral Busch pulled the aft emergency chain, thereby flushing the Golden Behind down the Tigris River. As the attack failed, an angry Dewey was heard to yell at his nephew, "D#$ your hide Curly, full court martial ahead for you!"

**Damn the torpedoes, full speed ahead!**

ADMIRAL DAVID FARRAGUT-1864

## ASSAULT ON BAGHDAD!

Illustrated by Jim Coon

      With the failure of the naval attack by Admiral Dewey Busch and Seaman Curly Busch on Baghdad, an enraged Field Marshal Von Toasty Franks-Hamburger orders an all out Blitzkrieg on the capital city by the U.S. Army, Marine Corps, and Air Force. The result is a bloodbath of destruction, as the city is pulverized in a punishing attack by the full weight of massive U.S. Military forces, who show off the awesome American military strategy of-Socks and Smell (meaning sniff out and destroy the enemy with stinky tactics). The wrecked city would surrender within a week. The Great Dictator could not be found in his bunker headquarters; it was assumed by U.S. Intelligence that he had gone underground into hiding. Before his forces could completely mop up the shocking smell of the city, Field Marshal Von Beans Franks-Hamburger had to leave his army to address another more frightening and fatal problem-an insubordinate general over at the Little Big Oil Well named George Hannibal Busch!

**The only good Iraqi, is a dead Iraqi!**

FIELD MARSHAL BLOODY VON BUSCH-2104

## NEW SHERIFF IN TOWN!

Illustrated by Jim Coon

When General George Busch did not obey Field Marshal Von Toasty Franks-Hamburger's orders to march on Baghdad with the 4th Cavalry Regiment in support of the final assault, the top commander arrived at the Little Big Oil Well from his headquarters with military police to arrest George for court martial on insubordination charges. Curly Busch managed to warn his brother by radio before the Field Marshal's arrival while out on a scouting patrol and observing the approaching commander's convoy through his binoculars. General Busch immediately placed an emergency call to his Ex-Daddy President, who in turn contacted the Vice President about the tense situation. General Busch was later rescued by the Secretary of Defense, who arrived at the oil well upon orders received by the Vice President with some members of the C.I.A.. They proceeded to arrest Field Marshal Von Toasty Franks-Hamburger on charges of incompetence instead. A grateful General Bloody Busch was released from previous arrest, and instructed by the Secretary of Defense that the 4th Cavalry could stay at the oil well to pursue the more important strategy of profiteering, instead of supporting the Army's final assault on Baghdad.

**'How far is St. Helena from the field of Waterloo?'**
**A near way-a clear way-the ship will take you soon.**
**A pleasant place for gentleman with little left to do.**

RUDYARD KIPLING-1892

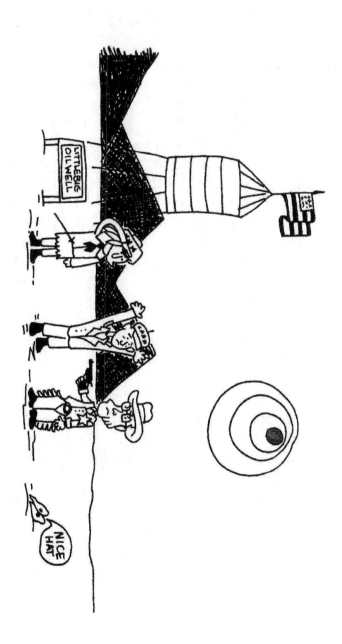

## SUPER HERO!

After the Secretary of Defense departed the Little Big Oil Well with the arrested Field Marshal Von Toasty Beans Franks-Hamburger, a happy General George Busch got down to the business of repairing battle damage, and reorganizing the Little Big Oil Well for profitable oil operations that would benefit his private family business and the U.S. Government. While engaged in this strenuous combat operation for patriotic duty, George received an unexpected and delightful visit from the Secretary of Defense a few weeks later. The secretary had arrived at the Little Big Oil Well upon orders received from the Vice President, to award Bloody Busch for opportunism beyond the call of duty, the U.S. Military's most prestigious medal of the 22$^{nd}$ Century-The Medal of Oil! Corporal Curly Busch acknowledges his brother as the general receives the award from the Secretary of Defense, with a universal salute of respect during the sacred ceremony.

**Next to a battle lost, the greatest misery is a battle gained.**

DUKE OF WELLINGTON- 1815

**Next to a battle lost, the greatest misery is my brother winning a great battle in a hopeless war!**

SGT. CURLY BUSCH-2108

**When you have to let the bean's gas go, let it out with all your might and power!**

SIR HAROLD FART STACEY/SYRACUSE, NY-1990

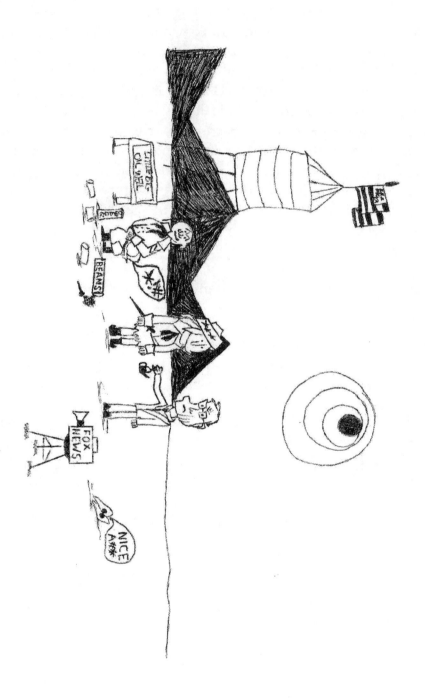

## SECTION III: IRAQ POST-WARS AND OCCUPATION CARTOONS

## ARBEIT MACHT FREI (WORK MAKES FREEDOM)!

After Operation Enduring Oil Supply was concluded, Field Marshal Von Busch concentrated on the business of occupying the conquered Iraq for the glory of the American Corporate Economic Empire. The Neo-Conservative George's main concern was to operate and maintain the Little Big Oil Well for the U.S. Government and personal profit. One clever method of profit-making was to employ, as cheap labor at the well, former captured members of the Iraq Republican Guard. This included the former captured Ex-Great Dictator of Iraq himself, whom Bloody Von Busch employed as the oil well's custodian. This cheap slave labor was only a fraction of paid wages that would be paid to the Liberated Iraq workers or foreign labor.

**Realpolitik-The use of military force to further a nation's material interests.**

GERMAN POLITICAL SCIENCE-19<sup>th</sup> CENTURY

## HIDE AND SEEK!

Immediately after the fall of Iraq, the Great Dictator fled Baghdad and went into hiding. Some experts had thought he had fled the country to seek asylum in another friendly Arab Country, while others thought he was simply hiding in the wastelands and deserts of Iraq. General George Busch was too busy with oil profits at the Little Big Oil Well to concern himself with this mystery, until one day when he had a heated argument with his brother Curly, something extraordinary happened. In a fit of rage over a sarcastic comment that Curly made, George angrily chased his brother out of the oil well and in the process almost fell into an oil hole in the desert. The oil hole was hiding none other than the Ex-Great Dictator of Iraq. Bloody George pulled his pistol, and the greatest non-captured prize in Iraq was now his! George now had possession of the two most valuable assets of Iraq.

### Asia is not big enough for two kings!

ALEXANDER THE GREAT-331 B.C.

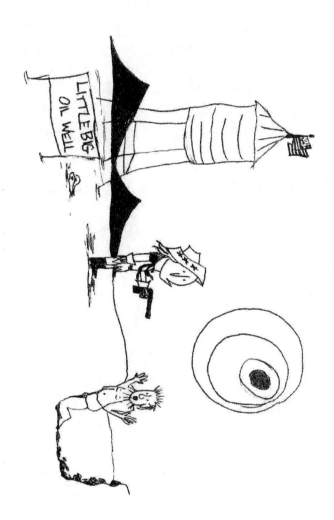

## PARTY-TIME!

Upon the capture of the Ex-Great Dictator, General George Hannibal Busch was promoted by high command on the recommendation of the Vice President to Field Marshal. George's capture of the former Iraq leader made him an instant bigger hero in the eyes of the American Media and general public. Bloody Busch, with the blessings of his Ex-Daddy President, took the aristocratic title of Von in order to elevate his social status with American High Society for possible future political aspirations. Field Marshal Von Busch then celebrated his good fortune with a cookout at the Little Big Oil Well of grilled foods and tasty beer.

**An army marches on its stomach.**

NAPOLEON BONAPARTE-1800

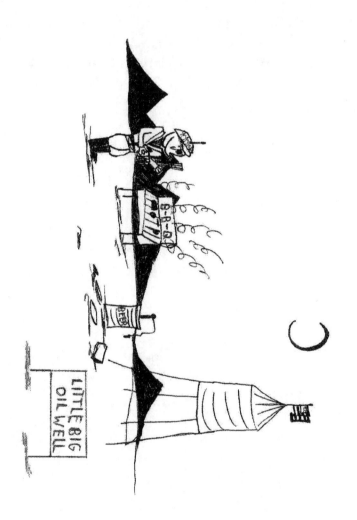

## PRIVATE BUSINESS!

Field Marshal Von Busch proceeds to turn the Little Big Oil Well into a private enterprise to increase the Busch Family's business holdings and assets. George's Ex-Daddy President supports him by gaining the approval of the Vice President to allow the Field Marshal to illegally supplement his military income with good old capitalist opportunism. This profitable business will maximize family profits from the black gold of Iraq's most prized oil well. Bloody Busch hires the Ex-Great Dictator of Iraq as cheap labor to manage the newly constructed Busch Corporation office building's parking lot, and other menial duties.

**To the victor go the spoils!**

BRENNUS-390 B.C.


**To the Loser, comes all the B.S.!**

SGT. CURLY BUSCH-2107

## NEW FORTRESS!

Once Field Marshal Von Busch had completed setting up his profitable private business at the Little Big Oil Well, he was awarded another honor and promotion. The Secretary of Defense orders George to Baghdad to assume command of all U.S. Military Forces occupying Iraq. The previous commander was Field Marshal Von Toasted Beans Franks-Hamburger, who had been relieved of command for incompetence for failing to capture Baghdad quickly enough. Critics charged that if Field Marshal Von Busch had supported him properly with his 4th Cavalry Regiment in the assault, Baghdad would have fallen sooner. Rumors also persisted that Von Franks-Hamburger's attempted arrest of an insubordinate Von Busch did not sit well with the bosses in Washington D.C.. Nevertheless, these charges were swept under the carpet as Bloody Von Busch arrived in Baghdad and built a new fort there for his headquarters.

**I hereby designate Berlin, as Fortress Berlin!**

ADOLF HITLER-1945

## CAMEL HUNTING!

The Vice President paid a visit to Iraq so he could inspect Field Marshal Von Busch's new fortress, and meet the troops for the Iraq occupation.  When the inspecting and business were over, George invited his father's pal out to the desert for some recreational camel hunting.  However, during the hunt the boss accidentally shot the wrong target....

**The only good Arab, is a dead Arab!**

FIELD MARSHAL BLOODY VON BUSCH-2104

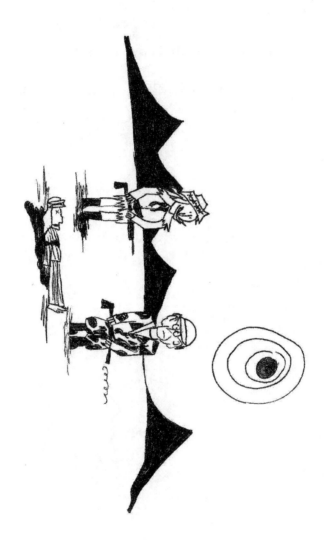

## CALIFORNIA, HERE I COME!

Following the hunting accident in the desert with the Vice President, the U.S. Media converged on the American leader after rumors leaked out about the incident from the Iraq hunting guides. When the press demanded answers and the truth about the event, the clever Field Marshal Von Busch initiated a covert cover-up in order to protect his boss. George and his 4th Cavalry Regiment entourage testified that the Iraq person shot was a dangerous terrorist from the El Quack's Terrorist Group of the World's #1 Terrorist. Of course, the unfortunate victim was really just one of the hunting guides. After the incident died down, a grateful Vice President rewarded his favorite general with extended leave time from his top post in Iraq. Von Busch took full advantage of this privilege, and headed for Hollywood with the Ex-Great Dictator to direct the future blockbuster film-**THEY DIED WITH THEIR OIL BOOTS ON!** This movie would recount the Hollywood Neo-Conservative version of Bloody Von Busch's epic victory at the Little Big Oil Well.

**Crush your enemies; see them driven before you, and to hear the lamentation of their women!**

ARNOLD SCHWARZENEGGER as CONAN- UNIVERSAL STUDIOS, 1981

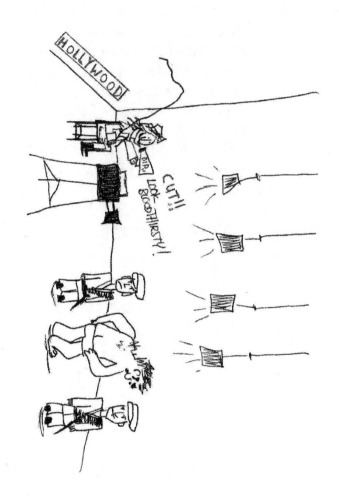

### THE GREAT TRIAL!

Field Marshal Von Busch returned to Iraq with the Ex-Great Dictator to resume his position as commander of all U.S. Military Forces immediately after completion of his magnificent propaganda film. Soon afterwards, George is instructed by the Vice President to place the Ex-Great Dictator of Iraq on trial for war crimes against humanity, in order to appease and satisfy World Liberal opinion. The result is a show trial in Baghdad with a kangaroo courtroom, where the defendant is acquitted of all charges except for one! The one charge he is found guilty of is simply disturbing the peace in Iraq. The warlord judge hands out a convenient light sentence whereby the Ex-Great Dictator will re-pay his debt to Iraq Society by working as a cheap slave laborer for the Busch Oil Corporation, for many years to come!

**Only a king may slay a king!**

ALEXANDER THE GREAT-329 B.C.

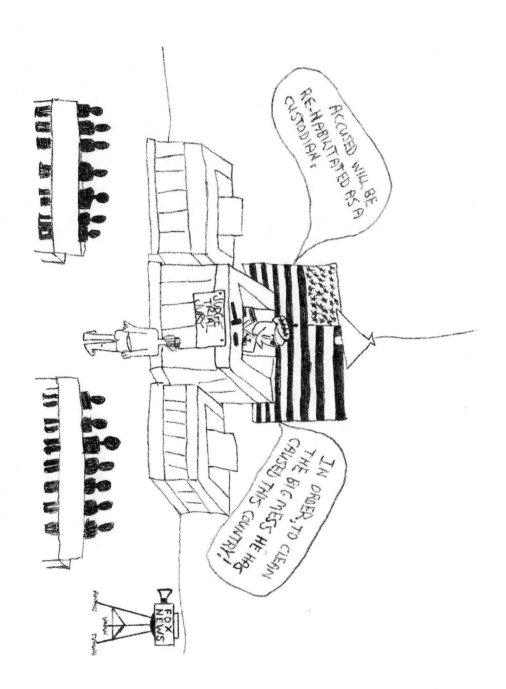

## BIG-BIG BUSINESS!

Field Marshal Von Busch assists the Vice President in building the boss's new major U.S. Corporate office building in Baghdad. George will provide the military security for the immensely profitable enterprise. The Ex-Great Dictator had left the Little Big Oil Well, to provide the slave labor for the dirty menial tasks of the new building. Bloody Von Busch then hired the former Iraq General Crazy Camel to do the vacated menial labor jobs at the oil well.

**We are now bigger than U.S. Steel!**

MEYER LANSKY-1950

**My brother and I are now smaller than General Motors!**

SGT. CURLY BUSCH-2108

88

## FUN TORTURE!

Once Field Marshal Von Busch assumed command of all U.S. Military Forces in Iraq, he began to aggressively pursue a national policy of ruthlessly crushing a growing rebellion by the Iraq people. The rebel insurgents included patriots, Muslim fanatics, former supporters of the Ex-Great Dictator and foreign mercenaries of the World's #1 Terrorist. In this growing guerrilla war, Bloody Von Busch builds a special notorious prison to hold and torture all the captured political prisoners. Upon its completed construction, the brutal George stands next to his scandalous military prison, which is aptly named-Ass-Grabbing Prison!

**War is cruelty, and you cannot refine it.**

WILLIAM TECUMSEH SHERMAN-1864

## ENEMY TORTURE!

In the U.S. Military occupation of Iraq, the notorious El Quack's Terrorist Group of the World's #1 Terrorist enjoy torturing their captives by gruesome decapitation. Very few of the captured Americans in Iraq, whether military or civilian, survive this horrifying fate. Likewise, in the U.S. Corporate Occupation of America, corporate terrorists conduct profitable torture by surgically removing the brains of future submissive politicians.

**War is fun, and everybody wants some more!**

SGT. CURLY BUSCH-2109

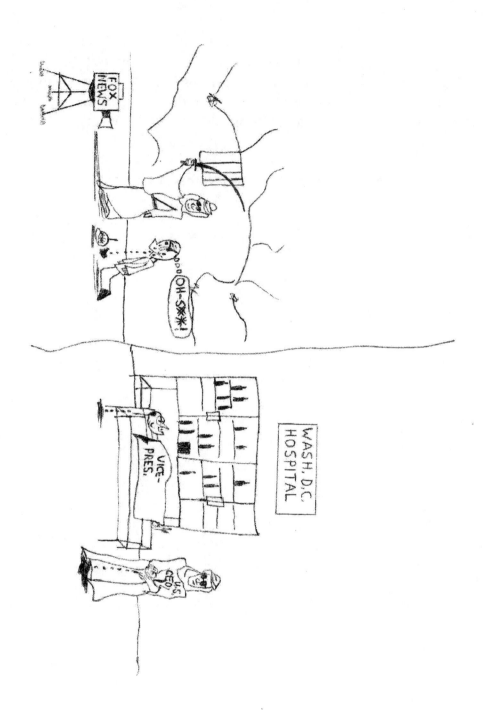

## THE BUTCHER OF BAGHDAD!

Field Marshal Bloody Von Busch declares martial law in Baghdad as the violent rebellion by Iraq insurgents and foreign terrorists spirals out of control. A sharp increase in ambushes and bombings of Iraq Civilians and American Military Forces, leads George to this desperate measure. Bloody Busch orders a brutal lock down on the city by strong U.S. Military Units, in order to safeguard American Corporate Business and his own private oil company in Iraq.

**Where my army rides, no grass grows!**

ATTILA THE HUN-452 A.D.

## THE WARLORD STANDS BEFORE CONGRESS!

As the months roll by, American Society becomes more impatient and disillusioned on the progress and conclusion of the U.S. Military Occupation in Iraq. Overall casualties and destruction from enemy attacks continue to rise at an alarming rate, even with martial law declared by Field Marshal Bloody Von Busch. Upon orders from the Vice President to appear before a Congressional investigative hearing on the Iraq dilemma, George gives his honest assessment on the progress of the Iraq Occupation and status of his military forces attempting to quell the rebellion.

**I always held my brother's truths to be self-envious and ambitious!**

SGT. CURLY BUSCH-2108

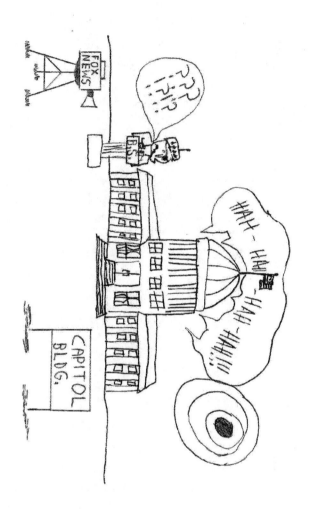

## SECTION IV: PRESIDENT GEORGE BLOODY VON BUSCH CARTOONS

## NOMINATED!

In 2107, Field Marshal Bloody Von Busch resigned from the U.S. Army and gave up his post as commander of all military forces in Iraq. The reason was to become a civilian, and run for the Presidency of the United States as the Republican Party Candidate. George's popularity as the great war hero in Iraq, and his brutal style of command over the occupied Iraq Nation gave him a lot of popularity in America for a run for the Oval Office. Of course, it did not hurt that his father was an Ex-President and the current Vice Presidential Leader would be behind him with their full support and power. The following year in 2108, George easily won the nomination to run for U.S. President at the Republican Convention held in Baghdad. Later that year, George was elected President in an extremely controversial and close election against the Democratic Party Candidate, who was always a bore!

**No one has ever seen a Republican mass meeting that was devoid of perception of the ludicrous.**

MARK TWAIN-1884

98

## TROUBLE IN THE BEDROOM!

In early 2109, President Von Busch moved into the White House and took his place as the American Supreme Leader in the Oval Office. In order to relieve the challenging and monumental task of administrating the American Corporate Economic Empire, George decided to re-live the past honeymoon with his wife in the White House's bedroom during their first night in their new home. Instead, Mr. Von Busch received an earful of nasty comments from his ex-playmate wife, the voluptuous Barby Von Busch. She proceeded to scold George for manipulating her sexy looks to enhance his voting total with the male and lesbian voters in the previous presidential election. The angry tirade by his wife, left the President as listless later in bed as the progress of the current Iraq Occupation!

**War is like sex, it's exciting-but ridiculous!**

SGT. CURLY BUSCH-2108

## BUDDIES!

During the first year of his reign, President Bloody Von Busch has a grand dream that reflects his rise to glory and power. In the dream, George confronts and acknowledges with respect his role model of the 20<sup>th</sup> Century-The Big Nasty Dictator!

**The Third Reich shall last 1000 years!**

ADOLF HITLER-1934

**The American Corporate Economic Empire will be lucky to last another 100 years!**

PRESIDENT BLOODY VON BUSCH-2111

**Today the book, tomorrow the world!**

SGT. CURLY BUSCH-2108

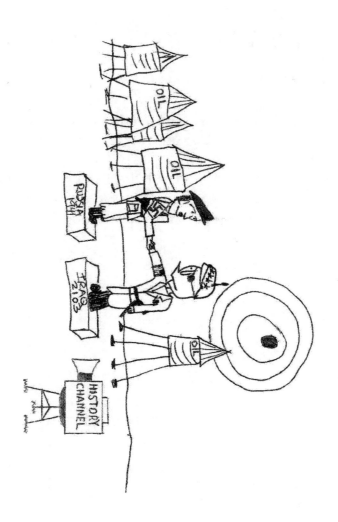

## TAKE ME OUT TO THE BALLPARK!

Illustrated by Jim Coon

In the springtime of 2109, President George Von Busch was invited by the Washington D.C. National Socialist's Major League baseball franchise to throw out the first pitch of the baseball season for the team and its fans. George heartily agreed to do this since he was a baseball fan, and former owner of the Texas Right-Wingers Major League team. He also viewed this event as another good way, like the White House bedroom, for relieving the stress of his demanding job and responsibilities. Opening day came, and Washington was playing Cleveland at home. President Bloody Von Busch arrived to start the game with a nice opening toss of the baseball to the National Socialist's pitcher. He also gave a rousing speech to inspire the whole National Socialist's team to defeat Cleveland. The rabid crowd of Washington fans roared, chanted, sang, and marched about their seats in precision order like political rallies held in Central Europe during the 1930's.....

**The only good Indian, is a dead Indian!**

GENERAL PHILLIP SHERIDAN-1870

## NEW BODYGUARD!

Later in the first year of his reign, the Neo-Conservative President Von Busch introduces his new security force to the American people, which will replace the Secret Service.  The idea for the new bodyguard is taken from the Nasty Dictator of the 20th Century, who employed his own personal and politically fanatical bodyguard in Nazi Germany.  Bloody Von Busch's new bodyguard will be hired mercenaries from Iraq-his fellow Republican buddies and former members of the Republican Guard. Any American Democrats, liberals, intellectuals, minorities, and any intelligent people left in the United States would have a very difficult time getting close to George to do any nasty deeds they might be secretly plotting to hatch.

### It's good to be the king!

MEL BROOKS as LOUIS XIV, HISTORY OF THE WORLD-20th CENTURY FOX, 1981

## F#$% THEM!

During the second year of his reign, President Bloody Von Busch throws a temper tantrum over his critic's statements on the progress of the Iraq Occupation. The first year of George's Presidency had been plagued by a worsening of America's Occupation in Iraq, from the military situation to the political and social. By the next year, the situation was becoming more desperate as observed by the Secretary of Defense and the Second Secretary of State-nicknamed the more bloodthirsty one, as they saw their boss's anger in action!

**L'etat c'est moi: je suis l'etat (The state is I; I am the state)!**

LOUIS XIV-1661

## OPERATION BIG SURGE!

During the third year of President Bloody Von Busch's reign, the situation in Iraq had deteriorated to the point where an overwhelming amount of American public opinion was against the U.S. Military continuing occupation. Tired of growing outspoken statements from critics all across America, George formulates a blood-thirsty military plan to end the Iraq Rebellion once and for all. The devious plan is simple-unleash a tidal wave of oil from the Iraq oil fields that will engulf and demolish Baghdad! The President hopes to evacuate all innocent Iraq citizens from the doomed city with the military, before the monstrous wave hits and drowns the terrorists and the insurgents, like the dirty rats they are!

## OIL'S UP!

SGT. CURLY BUSCH-2111

## WHERE'S MY F#$%^&* BOOT!

Hey, where the h#^& did all these f%$#*&@ Indians f^%$#@* come from!?

GENERAL CUSTER'S FAMOUS LAST WORDS-1876

What is General Custer most famous for?  Why he's the first man to wear a custom Arrow Shirt.

SGT. CURLY BUSCH-2103

## GENERAL CUSTER'S LOST BOOT!

Illustrated by Janan Driggers-2007

This boot was worn by General George Armstrong Custer when he was massacred with part of his 7th Cavalry Regiment at the Little Big Horn by hostile Indians in June of 1876.  The boot was located and retrieved near the general's dead body, by troops of General Terry's Command two days after the slaughter.  General Custer's other boot was rumored to have been stolen by Chief Crazy Horse as a war trophy.  Its whereabouts are unknown to this day.  The original boot drawn here is on display at the West Point Army Museum.

**I think'em we got our ass'em kicked good'em!**

LONE SURVIVOR OF CUSTER'S COLUMN-INDIAN SCOUT CURLEY, 1876

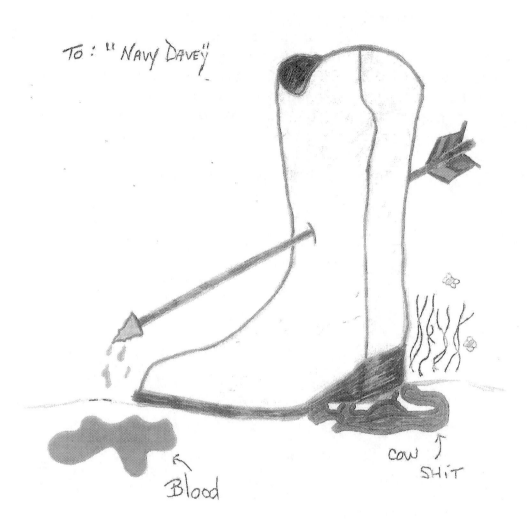

## SECTION V: BONUS STORY

## DAY OF THE CAMEL

The greatest terrorist attack in history was by the Serbian Black Hand terror gang. Their assassination of the Austrian Arch Duke Franz Ferdinand in 1914 directly triggered the beginning of W.W. I, and resulted in the deaths of over 20 million people! Maybe I can do better than this in the name of Allah!

ABDUL the MUSLIM-21st CENTURY

# DAY OF THE CAMEL
## A SHORT STORY
BY
DAVID L. CHISLING

## BY

## DAVID L. CHISLING

## I

There once was a massive urban center on Planet Earth called New York City. A man named Abdul the Muslim lived here. He was a devout Arab Muslim who had immigrated to the United States from Arabia when he was a young man. Like many immigrants to America, he settled in New York City. His dream was to become the classic American success story of the immigrant who someday owns his own business, and becomes financially independent and wealthy.

Abdul had honestly worked hard for thirty-five years to achieve the success he craved. He loved living in the United States, and the benefits of life in a Democratic country that offered so much opportunity for a foreigner like himself. At first, life was good to him in New York. Abdul established an export —import business thru Arabia with another Arabic partner. The business thrived, and he made a comfortable living that allowed monetary savings and future company expansion.

Abdul also gained his citizenship after seven years, and became an official American! Abdul married an Arabic woman who was an immigrant like himself. Life was momentarily blissful, as he settled down in a suburban house to raise children and live the, "American Dream." Abdul now viewed New York City as like the Islamic heaven that Allah had blessed him with.

Alas for poor Abdul the Muslim, by middle—age his good luck and blessing from Allah did not last. Starting about fifteen years after he had immigrated, and at the peak of his success, disasters befell him! The first problem was that recession hit the U.S. economy, and the business rapidly shrank in size and profits. Perhaps panicked by this change of fortune, Abdul's business partner stole most of the company's financial assets and fled back to Arabia, where he conveniently disappeared. Abdul was subsequently forced to declare bankruptcy, and lost his business to become instantly impoverished. This quickly placed a tremendous strain on his finances, and the stability of Abdul's marriage.

Abdul lived on unemployment and savings for six months, attempting to re—start his business with another partner or find a comparable job that matched his income from before. Unfortunately his efforts failed, and suddenly he was without unemployment and his savings became seriously depleted. Abdul would have no other option but humiliating himself, and take a low paying job to make ends meet to support his family.

Meanwhile, Abdul's wife who had been very loyal to him through several years of marriage started becoming impatient and hostile towards the man. She was too proud and spoiled as an Arabian Princess to tolerate her husband's sudden failures. Her loyalty to Abdul suddenly vanished, and she secretly decided that if his luck did not suddenly change; she would have no recourse but to leave him and seek a divorce! Abdul suspected nothing, and made the fatal mistake one day of insisting that she go to work also in order to finance the family's needs. This was too much for her to tolerate. She angrily denounced him, and informed Abdul she was taking the children and her valuables, and leaving him to go back to her family where she would seek an immediate divorce.

Abdul was too stunned and shocked to protest when she left the house. He only saw her and the kids once more, which was in divorce court. As soon as the marriage was legally dissolved, and she had taken most of his assets including the house, the woman returned forever to Arabia with the children. Abdul was left in the United States without a family, business, house, or savings. The only thing left to him was a minute checking account, a few personal possessions, a little furniture, and the used car with continual engine problems.

Abdul was now forced to live in a cheap apartment, within a low — income area of the city and experience the life of a low — wage worker living on a small income. This was a bitter blow to a man of honesty, pride, and faith in his Muslim Religion that had propelled himself to previous success. Over the next 15 years, Abdul the Muslim attempted to rebound and restore the things he had in the past. However; things only stayed the same and stagnated as he bounced from one low — paying job to the next through unfortunate circumstances. Abdul never re — married, and became isolated in his small dingy apartment over the years.

When Abdul the Muslim was an old man after living in America for a total of 30 years; he had changed into a frustrated and angry recluse. The only two things that kept his sanity were his, honest and simple faith in the goodness of Allah, and the mighty righteousness of American Democracy. Despite his past and present troubles, this simple virtuous man continued to live the life of an average honest citizen. A pretty amazing feat considering his living circumstances in the rat — race of the, "City That Never Sleeps." Nevertheless, things were about to quickly change as circumstances dictated that this passive angry man, suddenly turn into a person of profound action!

Abdul awoke in his run — down apartment one Sunday morning in early December. Abdul brushed a couple of cockroaches off his bed — sheets as he arose from bed. A rat scurried across the dirty, bare wooden floor as Abdul walked toward his holy blanket to kneel down in his underwear, and perform his morning Muslim prayers in the eastern direction of Mecca. Once finished with his prayers; he grabbed some clothes to dress in.

Abdul was slow in dressing, since he was now an older man who suffered from arthritis and bad knees. He was considerably overweight on his five — foot eight inch frame. This physical condition caused him to walk slowly and awkwardly. Abdul was also very pudgy, with a large waistline and a round fatty face. He had a large, prominent Semitic nose that was a bit curved. Over this, were two glaring brown eyes that radiated deep thought and wisdom. On top of his head was short black hair with a receding hairline that showed some graying hairs.

Once dressed, Abdul walked awkwardly from the apartment to buy a Sunday edition of the *New York Times* Newspaper. This was at a local deli shop that was owned by one of New York's most recent immigrant groups, the Koreans. In fact, the neighborhood that Abdul lived in was being overrun and taken over by them. So much so, that all shop and advertising signs were entirely in Korean. English was not to be seen, which made things confusing at times for non-Korean people like Abdul.

Abdul was not overly fond of the Koreans. Not because Abdul was a racist and bigot, because by nature he was not this type of person. It was simply that he knew from experience that some of them conducted crooked business deals, and everything in the neighborhood pertaining to them was to be, "Korean Only," at the exclusion of non-Koreans. Abdul noticed upon buying a paper from the Korean vendor, that the front headline news was about a major terrorist attack overseas that was committed by Muslim Arab Terrorists.

Upon returning to his dreary abode, Abdul made some tea to drink as he read the newspaper. Once it was ready, Abdul sat on his dilapidated couch to read the paper, as he drank the tea and smoked a cigar. Abdul spent the rest of the morning reading the newspaper, as he drank two cups of tea and smoked away on his big cigar.

The New York Times as usual, was full of articles pertaining to world political violence, corruption, and chaos. Headlining this week's news, was the never ending conflict between Israel and its Jews against the Palestinian Arabs and their Muslim Allies. Arab terrorists had struck against Israel in the largest, most horrifying and destructive attack to date. Over a thousand innocent people had died in a massive explosion from a huge terrorist bomb in the heart of one of Israel's major cities. Hundreds more had been wounded. Ironically, a small minority of those killed and wounded were innocent Palestinian Muslims. Abdul thought it sad and ironic that the Muslim terrorists had killed some of their own kind in order to strike at the Jews.

The rest of the world's bad news pertained to the ongoing political strife between races, nations, and social classes. The news was always the same as it had been for thousands of years of human history, only the names and places constantly changed. The depressing and dreary reading irritated and angered Abdul as it did on so many Sunday's before. Every Sunday morning, was basically a repeat of the Sunday before. By the time Abdul had finished reading the newspaper; he was ranting and raving how screwed up the world was.

Today was no exception, as Abdul went into a long and angry tirade about the evils of the world and his own personal condition, no doubt caused mainly by all non—Muslims. In particular, were certain groups that Abdul tended to despise owing to his Muslim beliefs.

Abdul angrily talked to himself as he shook his head, while finishing smoking his cigar and sipping the last of his cups of tea, "D@&* New York City Jews! They are without a doubt the most greedy, obnoxious people in this city. And they are so crooked to do business with, as I clearly remember from my days as a private businessman. They are rude and vulgar, and always looking for a way to rip you off in any business deal. They truly are the scourge of Allah! They are some of the reason I have been reduced to poverty for years, and cannot succeed in business in this city."

Abdul paused a moment as he collected his thoughts, before he shouted forth fresh tirades towards the American Jews, "And it is their support and fanaticism for Israel that causes our government to support that country against my Muslim brethren! They control the nation's press and media, so they can spread their vulgar propaganda to further their World Zionist cause. And their d@*&** money buys off and lobbies our politicians in Washington to strongly support Israel. And my Arab and Muslim brethren continue, and will continue to suffer under the yoke of greedy Zionist oppression and Imperialism. Why oh why does the great Democratic United States of America support such crooks and liars. That Allah, is the one and only thing that baffles me so much about this great country? Well, those Hebrews will get theirs someday; Allah will see to that!"

Abdul shook his fist into the air, as he walked angrily towards the window of his apartment to look at the street outside. His apartment was on the third floor, and Abdul could clearly see the numerous Korean businesses that dominated the neighborhood with their Korean Language signs.

"God D@** those Orientals," cried Abdul as he rose a fist towards the window as though possibly going to break it, "And those Infidels are crooked also, just like the Jews! They come in, take over through shady business, and dominate the neighborhood for their own kind. And much of their money goes back to Korea, not for the benefit of America and its citizens, just like the American Jew's money goes to Israel. They are undoubtedly shamed in the mind of Allah. And they will be condemned to everlasting Hell like the Jews too."

Abdul paused with his personal tirade, as he heard a commotion across the street coming from a local Catholic Church. It was one of the few white establishments left in the area, as this neighborhood in the past had been a predominantly Irish Catholic neighborhood. However; the bulk of the Irish had recently moved away for better neighborhoods, leaving the area for the newer immigrants coming into the city. The church, and a couple of pubs were all that was left of a former thriving community. At this moment, the last die—hard Irishmen in the neighborhood were leaving their last bastion of European Christendom.

"D@*& you heathen Christian Infidels too," shouted Abdul through the closed window that only a few outside pigeons might hear, "You are nothing more than the low—class white racists of Europe. You're in league with your cousin's the Jews, because of your false prophet, the Jew Jesus. Allah will see to it that you burn in Hell along with the Jews and Koreans. You're nothing but greedy, Infidel racists like your cousins the British."

Abdul became so upset by viewing the Irish Americans that he quickly opened his window and shouted as they stood on the church grounds and sidewalk.

"Go back to where you came from," yelled Abdul sarcastically as he prepared to close the window quickly in order to hide from view, "you come from nothing but the trash cans of Europe!"

Abdul quickly slammed shut the window and hid his head from view, so the Irish American people down below would not be able to locate him. After a minute, Abdul peeked out the window near its edge, and noticed the persons by the church peering about in confusion and anger. Abdul knew that nobody had located him, and he chuckled with hysterics as he discreetly moved away from the window to do other things.

As he picked the newspaper sections off the floor, and cleaned off his coffee table to empty his ashtray and wash his teacups, Abdul began another tirade.

"And speaking of those Irish people's cousins the British," cried Abdul as he threw pages of the newspaper violently into the trash, "May Allah throw them into eternal Hell also! Next to the Jews, they are the Devil's own people also. It was their empire that oppressed the world and my people, and kept us in great poverty for years. How the Muslims in Arabia and India suffered under those scoundrels so. Thank Allah, that their empire has crumbled and is no more. Praise Allah that the United States supported our independence movements against the Imperial British, and made us rich with the oil trade."

Abdul continued his personal discussion, as he shook his head in confusion, "I only wish that our great American Government would not ally themselves so closely with Britain like they do with Israel. How can people ally themselves with such Infidel scoundrels like those two? The very scourge and enemies of all mankind! Why not become friendlier with the Germans, since they were so nice to me long ago when I went to Berlin on a business trip when times were better. Despite the legacy and temporary horror of Adolf Hitler, I found the

Germans to be so much more warm and friendly than those cursed British and Jews."

"Praise be to Allah that many a good German in the last great war put a lot of the Brits and Jews into their graves, " mumbled Abdul to himself as he laughed sadistically, like a man who was truly beginning to go completely insane.

Next, Abdul in his speaking delirium walked to the center of the apartment and looked to the ceiling as he spread forth his arms to speak. He looked like a holy prophet of Islam communicating directly to Allah.

Abdul cried, "And d®** all white Christian Americans who are racists too. Especially the Republicans, since I am a die—hard Democrat who supports great liberal leaders like Bill Clinton was. Praise be to Allah that some Americans are as enlightened and pure of heart as our ex—President. As for our present President Bush, Allah d®*& him to Hell for his support of the conservative establishment that will bleed all us working people dry for their greed and decadent Infidel sins that they support. For under the leadership of the Republicans, this free society will be nothing more than a shambles of self—centered opportunism!!"

Abdul finally calmed down, stopped his angry self discussions and turned on the television to get his mind off depressing politics. Interestingly enough, Abdul watched a rerun of the, "Jerry Seinfeld Show." He totally enjoyed and laughed at it, which enabled him to successfully unwind. This being another amazing example of the American concept of cultural assimilation!

Over the following week, Abdul's anger that had surfaced Sunday over politics grew and became more intense. In the past, he could calm himself after his political tirades, and be quickly back to his normal self. This time however; things were different because he could not stop thinking about the problems of the world. As Abdul left his apartment on weekdays for work; his hidden anger boiled while exposed to non—Muslim persons at work and on the streets.

Meanwhile, everyday in the news there were new stories of more terrorist attacks worldwide by Arab Muslim terrorists of the Near East. It looked as though a world—wide terrorist war had suddenly started. This constant terrorist news only caused Abdul to become more agitated, and continued fueling his growing bigotry towards non—Muslim groups like the Jews and Koreans. On Friday, when Abdul returned to his apartment after finishing his job for the week, there was a special report on the television's evening news.

It was a report on the taped interview with the leading and most wanted terrorist in the world. It was strongly suspected by the United States that this Arab Muslim fanatic was behind last week's major bombing in Israel, and other attacks occurring worldwide this week. It was only a matter of time before the

American government expected him to strike directly at the United States. His taped speech before the interviewer's camera was propaganda that attacked Israel, and those in the world who supported it. The speech was not very different in its basic content from what Abdul had been raving about the previous Sunday.

The only different topic, was when the leading terrorist shouted into the camera, "And I now call upon all my Muslim Brethren, everywhere in the world, to join me in a war of Holy Jihad against all Infidels everywhere! Especially those Jews in Israel, and those Jews and Infidels in America who support the Little Satan of Israel. We will unite and sweep forth from Arabia through the Middle— East, and assist our brothers the Palestinians in wiping off the face of the Earth and eradicating the unholy state of Israel! Then we will turn our attention on the Great Satan of America itself, and launch a war of terror the world has not seen since the days of the Golden Horde and Genghis Khan!! Join with me brothers, and begin the Holy Jihad War today!

Abdul sat hypnotized and entranced by this call for Jihad from the leading world terrorist. He sat for an hour contemplating the renegade's message long after the news cast was finished. Abdul was impressed by the speech when he went to bed early that night, and the terrorist's dialogue was in the back of his mind the whole night. In fact, the subject was on his mind the complete weekend. It only increased his anger, hate, and intolerance against non-Muslims living in New York City.

Abdul's thoughts came to a climax by the end of the weekend. After reading the Sunday New York Times, and watching television news throughout the weekend that highlighted continual terror threats and attacks, Abdul finally snapped. He suddenly crossed the line from being a passive political observer, to an active participant! After Abdul had watched the news show, "Sixty Minutes," which was a special report on world—wide terrorist activities; he had made a firm decision that would forever alter the course of his life.

Abdul mumbled as he switched off the power button to the television, "Must stay calm and not talk loudly anymore. Cannot let the neighbors hear or suspect anything."

Abdul sat down in his dilapidated couch to smoke a cigar and meditate on what action to take. Abdul stated firmly in a low voice while puffing on a fresh cigar, "That's it. I Abdul the Muslim will heed the advice from the great Muslim terrorist who speaks directly from Allah's voice, and start a holy Jihad against the Infidels. For I will single-handedly plan and commit the most perfect terrorist attack right here in New York City.

It will be so good, that all eyes of the Muslim World and from Allah will be turned on me with great praise. I shall not survive this act, but, I will surely go down in Islamic History as a great hero and martyr. And I am sure to end up in

Allah's heaven, away from this Infidel Hell of New York City. The young virgins and wine will be waiting and flowing for me soon. And maybe my great act of bravery will hasten the day when the Great Jihad is won, and Islam will come to America and find root in the government, and American's will finally discover the grace of an Islamic State. No more of their heathen and barbaric notion of the separation of church and state like with the Jews in Israel. For this is the ultimate blasphemy before the eyes of God! Tomorrow, I begin and think up a plan of heroic action."

Upon releasing and organizing his inner political thoughts, plans, and desires; Abdul went to bed. There Abdul had the best night's sleep he had in a long time. For this was the clear conscious of the fanatical terrorist, now preparing to commit an act of righteous violence that would guarantee him entrance into Heaven.

The following day, a determined Abdul the Muslim started the week with his mind concentrating on his new—found profession of terrorist. While at work the next day, he formulated ideas and plans to organize and initiate the perfect terrorist attack. Arriving to his apartment that night, Abdul sat on his dilapidated couch after dinner with a cigar, contemplating the ideas he had been thinking of throughout the day.

Abdul quietly muttered as he puffed slowly on his soothing cigar, "I will act alone. I am my own terrorist group. That will help to ensure total secrecy. My code—name will be-—-.Camel. That is a fitting name, since it is the animal that is so closely associated with my kind by these Infidels of America. And the Camel is sneaky and smart, always underestimated by its owners and enemies. This is exactly how I will have to behave if I am to succeed in this dangerous enterprise. I do not expect to survive of course, since it will be a suicide bombing, and I will be the suicide bomber. I will commit this attack in the near future in a place that is easy to access, an area with multitudes of densely packed crowds, and it will be exposed to live television coverage in front of tens of millions of persons. What better way to achieve notoriety and obtain publicity. As well as the utter shock of it will heighten the nation's paranoia, and fear."

"As for the details," continued Abdul speaking as he took a deep puff on the smoky cigar, "I'll begin working on them tomorrow. I do know that I must quit my job at the middle of the month, so I can spend full time on this project before the expected deadline. I have plenty of money to get me into next month, so being unemployed will have no effect on me. And besides, I'll be dead soon, so, I won't have to worry about finding new employment or a source of income for the future."

Abdul now smiled deviously as he spoke with himself further, "Of course, I'll have to get hold of a bomb device with a detonator to commit the terrorist act. That shouldn't be too hard though, I can probably obtain any information I need from the New York City Library. And since I won't be alive or known upon my death after the act of terror is committed; I will mail out letters on the day of the attack explaining my identity and motives. I will send letters to the major newspapers, mayor's office, and the local police precinct. At least they will get a full run—down of who and why I did this, after all the panic and questions begin flying."

Abdul the Camel began implementing the details of his perfect terrorist attack the following day. The first thing he did was to quit his job in the morning, and by the afternoon he was at the city library obtaining information through books and computer on how to build a lethal home—made bomb. Abdul took careful notes on note—pad paper, since he did not want to arouse any suspicion by checking library materials out at the main desk.

By the middle of the month, Abdul had purchased the materials needed to construct a home—made bomb in his apartment. Being unemployed, he would have full ample time to build the explosive, and take care of other details that would ensure a successful operation. Abdul knew he should be ready by the end of the month to conduct his perfect terrorist operation.

By the end of December, Abdul had succeeded in building the suicide bomb, and had written several letters to be mailed the day of his terrorist act. Nobody had come into the apartment all month, because he lived as a recluse. Abdul had concealed the terrorist objects well, in case some uninvited guests like the landlord or thieves came into the premises without his permission. Christmas and the holiday season would not be a distraction for him, since as a Muslim he had never heavily involved himself in the Infidel Christian festivities of America.

December 31st finally came, and Abdul the Camel was ready to commit his perfect act of terrorism that very night! He stayed in the apartment all day, and fasted while doing his prayers diligently towards Mecca like a good Muslim. Abdul carefully assembled and laid out the clothes he would wear tonight on his bed. The bomb was placed on his dinner table, and the envelopes with the information letters were put on his writing desk.

Abdul quietly meditated all day in between his prayers. Abdul ate nothing, since he would die as a pure martyr with a soul cleansed of the want for food. Abdul also shaved much of his body hair off his skin and armpits, so he would die more pure. He cut and shaved his head bald, to further his purity for entering Islamic Heaven. Abdul also checked the bomb over carefully, to make sure the wiring and detonator would work properly so it would not be a dud. In the early evening, Abdul made ready to leave his apartment to commit the act of terror. First, he dressed himself with the clothes on the bed, which would be winter dress of black pants, shirt, and boots. Secondly, he took gray electrical tape, and taped his homemade bomb securely to his torso over the black shirt. Abdul would also wear a large black coat he had specially bought for the occasion that was loose fitting so that it would provide plenty of concealment for the bomb. His whole dress would be in black, so he could feel the effect of wearing the color that had been preferred by professional assassins the world over down the centuries from the Japanese Ninja to Arabic assassins.

Abdul was soon dressed, and put on the large bulky coat over the shirt that had the bomb taped to it. He looked quickly into the mirror to assure the coat fitted loosely enough to totally conceal the weapon. Satisfied that everything looked normal, and no suspicion would be aroused, Abdul placed a black Fedora hat on his head. He looked at himself again in the mirror and smiled.

Abdul stated to himself with amused satisfaction, "I'm not only wearing the colors of a professional assassin, but, I look like one of those Ultra — Conservative Jew males from Brooklyn. And if people at the target sight think the same, it is unlikely I will ever be suspected for what I really am before I detonate the terrorist device. How convenient!"

Abdul now grabbed the letters to mail, and stuffed the roll of electrical tape into a coat pocket, just in case the bomb became loose later and he would have to duck into a rest—room stall and re—tape it. Before leaving his apartment for the last time, Abdul bowed and did a quick prayer towards Mecca to allow blessing the habitat, and give good luck to accomplish the terrorist deed he was about to commit. Once finished, Abdul left his apartment, and headed for the subway station that would take him to Forty—Second street and Times Square for the yearly New Year's Eve celebration! Before entering the local subway station, Abdul mailed the information letters in a nearby mailbox so they would arrive to the right authorities after successfully completing his terrorist attack.

One hour later, Abdul arrived at the Forty—Second Street station in Manhattan by Times Square. The subway cars and station were packed with multitudes of people, converging on Times Square for the huge midnight New Year's celebration. Abdul left the subway car, and walked slowly and cautiously through the crowds in order not to jostle the bomb he was carrying under his coat too much. Besides, it was only mid—evening. Plenty of time to walk onto the streets, and eventually position himself in the center of the crowd later in the middle of the square.

Abdul was on the lookout for police, undercover detectives, and any type of private security guards that might be looking to bust an individual like himself. Abdul was smart enough to realize that he must be on guard from any astute citizen's alert enough to pick up on his illegal activity. But, as Abdul had planned, if he acted cool and harmless enough by blending into the crowd as another New Year's reveler; he should be lucky enough not to attract any undue attention.

So far, Abdul had only spotted some transit police in the subway system. It appeared there were only a little more on duty than usual. Abdul climbed the subway station stairs and exited onto the street at Broadway and Forty—Second Street. Hundreds to thousands of persons were already assembling and milling about the area in anticipation of the coming midnight festivities. The densely packed street was void of vehicles, since the police had already cordoned off the area to traffic.

Abdul could see police road blocks positioned at street intersections on the outside area of Times Square. The cops were watching the crowd carefully, ready to do anything necessary to control the mobs. Abdul quickly melted into the crowd that was moving along the sidewalk, and walked along quietly so as not to attract any attention from the watchful police. Meanwhile, the intense glare and reflection from the mass of neon signs overhead on the surrounding buildings glared down, and added a surreal atmosphere to the already abnormal pedestrian situation.

As Abdul started walking from the station down the street in the general direction of the center of Times Square; his gaze briefly beheld a tall white male standing at a corner of an adjacent building. The guy looked a bit suspicious, as he stood there eyeing the passing crowds intently from the corner of his eyes. Abdul suspected in the back of his mind that this person was possibly up to no good, or might even be a police undercover detective. His random gaze towards the man must have given his thoughts away, for the tall guy suddenly looked directly at him and gave a suspicious look as though communicating for Abdul to mind his own business. Abdul immediately took the hint and averted his gaze away from the person, and continued walking along the sidewalk minding his own business. After Abdul had passed the tall guy, the man stared at Abdul as though sizing and scrutinizing the Arab for some set purpose.

This suspicious guy that Abdul had momentarily spotted was none other than Steve the Pickpocket. Steve happened to be one of the best thieves of this particular specialty in the city. He loved working unsuspecting crowds of people, where he usually found his best business victimizing persons owing to the simple fact it was so easy to hide and become lost in the vast multitudes of people. The holidays were the best times, especially at Christmas and New Years when the most people were about. And the best time and place for stealing was always New Years on Times Square. There were no better victims than unsuspecting drunkards in a densely packed crowd, who were off guard to a professional such as Steve picking their pockets.

At this moment, Steve rubbed his hands together momentarily with glee while smiling, as he dreamed about the rich pickings he would obtain on this night.

"That Arab or Indian guy that just passed me," mumbled Steve to himself in such a way that other pedestrians might take him for just another kooky street person, "that sand turd better mind his own business. Even if he is maybe another pickpocket like me, they should deport his ass like so many others of these immigrants who are cluttering up my city. These petty foreign thieves simply take away business from me, and give me unneeded competition in addition to a worse rap, because of the extra crime and legal hassles they create. The H*&$ with them all! Shoot their a@*&*.ht

Abdul could not have encountered anybody more incompatible, and hostile to himself than Steve on this festive night in Times Square. For Steve was Abdul's worse Infidel nightmare! Steve was a white Irish — American who was a native of New York City, having been born and raised here as a Catholic. Steve came from a conservative family that was die — hard Republican, so he intensely disliked all Democrats. He was very racist towards people who were non — white, and not Christian. Steve was even a little hostile towards white people who were not of Irish descent. He especially detested Jews, Arabs, and Indians, and their different religions did not matter. He hated them all equally.

Even physically, Steve was the opposite of Abdul. He was younger, being in his mid — thirties. Steve was a tall guy, and fairly lean and muscular despite having a bit of a beer gut. He had short, black hair that was prematurely balding with a small amount of graying hairs. Steve had blue eyes, and a few freckles dotting his cheeks. He liked to wear expensive clothes, even when engaged in crime. Steve felt this would make people respect and trust him more, therefore making it easier to catch persons off guard in order to victimize them.

Steve was dressed in a long, heavy fur coat designed for winter weather. Steve wore nice green dress pants, and had expensive trendy sneakers on his feet. These white and black sneakers were far better than shoes in plying his trade, since if he was chased by cops for pick-pocketing, it would be much easier to escape and run in these than dress shoes. Steve also had an expensive pair of black leather gloves that he would conveniently place in a coat pocket once it was time to pickpocket somebody and use his crafty and nimble fingers.

Steve was very handsome, and many members of the opposite sex found him attractive. He would take advantage of this, and have non — serious affairs with loose women that did not last long. Steve smoked cigarettes heavily, and was a chain smoker. He ironically smoked Camels, which was of course the code name for Abdul's one man terrorist group.

Steve needed the Camels constantly, just as he did alcohol, since alcohol abuse was an important facet of his life. These substances calmed his high — strung nerves since his life had been tumultuous and dangerous. Steve came from a broken home, and had quit high school to join the military. Later, he was thrown out of the Army for attitude problems and incompetence. With no career job or future, Steve had turned to petty crime such as pick-pocketing in order to make a living and survive.

Steve managed to make a pretty decent living from this, when he was not in and out of jail, which was where he had spent much time the last five years. Overall, Steve was one of life's losers, plagued by addictions to gambling, booze, spending money, drugs, and sexual relations with undesirable women. But, Steve was a survivor, and he had planted himself at Times Square to survive another day with a little more wealth and money.

Steve suddenly grew restless, and left his observation corner of the building to begin moving with the crowd towards the center of the square and its action. Steve did not realize that because of some twist of fate; he was heading in the precise direction that Abdul had taken. Steve would also have been a bit amused to understand that Abdul and himself did have two things in common politically. The first was they both hated Jews. The second was that they both detested the British, and their former mighty empire. The reason of the Brit dislike was easy for Steve, since his family was predominantly Irish-American, although there was a little English blood in his family's background.

Both Steve and Abdul made their way steadily towards the center of Times Square over the next hour, amidst the ever – expanding mass mob of New Year's revelers. In this time, Steve made a couple of successful pickpockets that nabbed him a wallet and its contents, plus the contents of a purse. Not a bad start, for what should become a profitable evening.

Meanwhile, Abdul was patiently and steadily moving his way through the massive crowds to the best position possible for initiating an act of terror. He had spotted many city cops on the fringes of the crowd, and at street intersections. Abdul was careful to avoid walking too near them, or make any direct eye contact. As he moved farther into the dense crowd at the center of the square however; the police became far fewer, since it obviously became impossible for them to observe and operate properly in such a densely packed mass of people. Abdul knew at this point, the only thing he had to fear was from undercover detectives blending in with the crowd, or police observers overhead who were observing the crowd from building windows or helicopters.

The final position that Abdul wanted to blow the bomb, from, was as near as possible toward the live telecast crew that always hosted this event on national television. It was also important to center himself in the middle of the square, so the blast would have the most devastating effect on the tightly compacted masses of people. Abdul had planned and knew, that the greatest shock effect of his terrible action would be the fact that it was televised live, to tens of millions of people. What better way to send a political message, and spread the cause of Islam, than to commit a mass terrorist attack on live media that was witnessed by countless viewers as it occurred. Abdul knew that he would go down in Arab History as a great hero, and would win a huge victory in the war of the Muslims over the Infidels!

Eventually after much patience and jostling, Abdul managed to position himself in the desired spot. The time was a quarter to eleven, a little over an hour before the magic moment of midnight. Once positioned, Abdul felt confident that everything was going perfect according to plan. Abdul scanned the area immediately adjacent to him, and saw no cops or suspicious looking persons in the vicinity.

The only thing Abdul sensed wrong at this moment, was that it felt as though the bomb inside his coat had become loose under the tape. The bumping and moving through the crowds the last couple of hours had undoubtedly loosened the tape covering that wrapped around the weapon. Abdul simply hoped that the tape job would hold until midnight, since it was impossible to find a rest—room at this point for repair, without losing his ideal position in the crowd. And he could not very well open his coat to fix the tape, since countless people were too closely packed against him, making it impossible to use his arms in such an endeavor. And besides, he would be risking the chance that some astute spectator might observe and register that he was carrying a suspicious looking object, and alert security. Abdul then might not even have a chance to finish the attack, and would simply be apprehended and carted off to jail.

Abdul took a deep breath to calm himself, and stood waiting for twelve—o'clock to arrive. He immediately mixed in with the crowd by yelling enthusiastically, and waving his arms on occasion in celebration. Abdul had cleverly figured that if he stood quietly motionless until midnight, this might attract attention from unwanted eyes for unnatural behavior. So, he tried to behave like the other revelers, just hoping not to overdo it where the bomb might be damaged or misplaced under his coat. In the meantime, Steve the Pickpocket was not far away in the mob, looking for fresh victims of crime.

It was not long before an hour had passed, and the Times Square clock read a quarter to twelve. Abdul was still in proper position with the bomb. Everything had gone well for him, the bomb still felt secure under his coat and he had not noticed any suspicious persons around him in this time. In the meantime, Steve was nearby roaming the crowd. In the last hour, Steve had picked three more victims for wallets, jewelry, and purse contents. The crowd was so densely packed with roving eyes, that like Abdul, Steve dared not view and examine the items he had just pilfered and hid in his coat.

As midnight approached, the crowd became more restless and festive. The noise level became stupendous with yelling, cheering, and noise from celebration toys that people carried. Adding to the volume was the background noise of sirens, police radios, police and television helicopters, music, policemen yelling through megaphones and the television personalities analyzing the crowd. In addition to this, was the surreal affect of the entire spectrum of neon signs emanating from the densely packed buildings nearby.

A special white ball light, with its long rod stood ready for dropping to measure the last thirty seconds of the old year. All this activity was constantly being reported by live television through the celebrity hosts that sat not far from Abdul above ground in their reporting booth. The celebrities cheerfully and humorously commented on the festivities, never sensing or suspecting that in the crowd there now stood a secret terrorist about to commit the most heinous live act of terror in history.

Suddenly, the time was eleven—fifty—five and Abdul mentally prepared himself for action at precisely midnight. His attitude became focused on his deed, as he briefly rubbed his coat with one hand to verify the bomb was still there and securely in place. It was still loose from his movements during the night. Abdul breathed a sigh of relief at the condition of the bomb, as he took his gloves off and carefully placed them in the coat pocket over the roll of electrical tape hidden there earlier, in case needed for re—taping the weapon to his torso. No suspicious persons looked to be around, as Abdul made a quick scan of the crowd near him.

The only sign of nervousness that Abdul displayed, which a keen observer may have noticed was that he was sweating profusely. Abdul did not even feel or notice this, since he was so obsessed and occupied with carrying out his mission. As it was, Abdul need not have feared this minor display of suspicion, since the persons pressed tightly about him were too preoccupied with the holiday celebration to notice anything. And Abdul was too well hidden in the crowd for security or police, to notice any suspicious behavior from him, unless he was being observed from above. Which in that case, there was nothing Abdul could do about it. He would just have to trust in the luck of Allah to finish his heroic act. As it was, Abdul had nothing to fear, since at this moment he was just another New Year's reveler among hundreds of thousands, whom the police never suspected and were not directly watching.

Suddenly, it was a minute towards midnight, and the crowd went wild with delight as loud noise and cheering deafened the air. The noise was so loud, that it muffled the voices of the celebrities in the television booth who were hosting the celebration. Abdul stood quiet and motionless, with sweat pouring down his forehead as he concentrated on opening his coat so he could reach into it and activate the detonator button on the bomb. At this point, he did look suddenly suspicious in the crowd. However; unfortunately nobody was or would pay any attention to him, since all people in Times Square, including many of the authorities, were completely preoccupied with the stroke of midnight.

As Abdul finished opening his coat, and placed a hand carefully inside to feel for the explosive device, it was thirty seconds before midnight. The magnificent white lighted ball began traveling down its pole towards the bottom, where in thirty seconds it would officially announce the start of a new year. The huge crowd screamed and roared extra loud again with deafening effect, as the lit ball started moving. Abdul proceeded to locate the bomb device by hand, as he had done many times before, practicing at home with the bomb concealed inside his coat. He had learned to simulate blowing the bomb without looking directly at it, since this would arouse less suspicion, and help keep the weapon away from unwanted eyes during its future use.

Abdul soon had his hand on the bomb's detonator part, and a finger carefully pushed the switch that activated the bomb. The only thing left now was to push the button that would trigger the explosion, and end his life and others around him for the glory of Mohammed and Allah. This would be in precisely fifteen seconds! At this point, a great sense of victory and joy surged through Abdul's mind and body since he knew that unless the bomb itself was defective and failed to explode; he would succeed in committing the perfect terrorist attack against the hated Infidels! Abdul now carefully began moving a finger towards the explosion button, where he would position it very lightly, to press it at exactly to the second at midnight.

Abdul suddenly received the shock of his life, as his finger never arrived exactly at the detonator button. This was that his hand found and felt another hand obstructing the way! He looked down in sudden panic, and noticed an arm from another person sticking into his coat. Abdul quickly looked to the side, and saw a tall white male standing there who looked oddly familiar, but at this instant of crises he could not instantly recognize the guy. The unwanted and undesirable person that Abdul saw, was none other than Steve the Pickpocket!

Unknown to Abdul, he had been watched by Steve recently, but for an entirely different reason than suspicion of a plot to commit terrorism. It was simply to victimize Abdul in an act of petty thievery. For at precisely four minutes to twelve, immediately after Abdul had scanned the crowd one last time for suspicious persons; Steve had randomly stumbled across him while looking for more victims in the mass celebration. Steve was luckily behind and to the side of Abdul, so he was well concealed from Abdul's view. Steve immediately recognized Abdul from earlier in the evening, and instantly decided from the guy's previous behavior, that something valuable must be hidden in the coat! In a split second, Steve decided he would arrive near Abdul from behind, and pick his pocket at exactly midnight, when the crowd's hysteria would reach a fever pitch and cause the most distraction.

In the rest of the little time before midnight, Steve carefully moved and positioned himself in the dense crowd directly behind an unsuspecting Abdul. At precisely thirty seconds to midnight, Steve looked down and started moving his hand to the side of Abdul's coat. Nevertheless, before his hand came close to the coat; one of Abdul's hands unbuttoned the large coat. Steve was startled, but did not panic or give up in the pickpocket operation. This was because he instantly knew that Abdul was probably reaching into his coat to grab a camera for taking a picture at midnight. And since it was a night picture in this wild setting, only a special and expensive camera could successfully take a good picture. Great for stealing! And it further exposed Abdul's pants more readily that he could slip one hand inside the coat to steal his wallet from a pant's pocket, and at the same time grab the camera with his other hand directly from Abdul's hand. Then it would be easy to quickly move off and become lost in the crowd before Abdul could pursue him or raise the alarm for help. It would be a perfect heist, two expensive items at once, making the night a very profitable venture indeed!

Steve was professional and experienced enough, that he could instantly observe, plan, and carry out this special heist in a matter of seconds. Which was precisely what had happened when he deftly and quickly slipped a hand inside the coat several seconds before mid—night, and prepared the other hand to snatch Abdul's supposed camera at precisely the instant that he lifted Abdul's wallet from the pant's pocket to outside the coat. Everything went according to plan, until Steve's hand rubbed against another hand inside the coat. Steve instantly froze his movements, as Abdul turned and stared at him in alarm and shock. Steve immediately knew in a split second that he had made one fatal miscalculation. This was that because of standing behind his victim, he had assumed Abdul had pulled a camera out of the coat. Steve had never seen anything with his eyes, so he had no idea that the guy's hand was still positioned inside the coat. Certainly a stupid error, but, you did not become a truly successful pickpocket unless you made assumptions and took chances on occasion.

Steve made the instantaneous decision to withdraw his hand with lightening speed, and run off to escape any further problems that would lead to his apprehension by the police. As Steve moved his hand away; he did wonder in the back of his mind that it was odd that the guy had kept his hand inside the coat, when he must have unbuttoned it to retrieve something. This odd thought was suddenly erased from his mind as Steve realized his pulled hand was not going anywhere. This was that Abdul had instinctively brought his other hand up, and gripped Steve's wrist to pull the pickpocket's hand away so his other hand could finish pushing the detonator button to blow them all up.

The result was a short intense scuffle, as Steve attempted to break his hand free from Abdul's grasp, and Abdul tried to detonate the weapon in an instant, Steve brought his other hand to his forearm and yanked his trapped hand violently backwards, to help break Abdul's grasp of his restrained hand. At the moment Steve's arm yanked back forcefully, and his hand finally broke free from Abdul's grasp; Steve's resistance caused his hand to swipe the side of the bomb. The force of this swipe managed to knock the weapon off Abdul's torso, mainly because the tape holding it had become loose and weak. As Abdul finally brought his hand's finger down to push the detonate button, while using his other hand to struggle with Steve, the trigger finger found nothing but air! That was because the bomb had already dropped from his body and was clattering on the ground. Abdul's finger had missed the detonate button by a mere quarter of an inch before it fell!!

Abdul looked down quickly in frustration and panic, with the intent of kneeling down and still instantly pushing the detonate button. That is, if the bomb still worked after the fall. Meanwhile, other persons directly adjacent to Abdul were watching him and Steve, because of the commotion of the scuffle. They clearly saw a strange object fall from Abdul's coat onto the ground. At the same time, Steve pulled his freed hand back and made ready to run and escape as fast as possible into the dense crowd. Nevertheless, he too saw a strange object fall from Abdul's coat. Before Steve began running; he paused a second and looked at this strange object clattering on the ground near Abdul. Owing to his experience as a criminal and dealing with the underworld; Steve knew immediately what this object looked like. He now made the most momentous choice of his life——run like H*$& to save himself if this weird madman was serious about blowing this thing if it was real, or, stay and attempt to confiscate the weapon and prevent this clown from detonating it!

"Grab that guy, screamed Steve as loudly as he had ever done in his life, "he's got a bomb! Stop him before he blows it!!"

Luckily for the people of Times Square and the American Government, Steve despite his shady reputation and improper profession, decided to play the hero for once and save lives. He jumped down towards the bomb to prevent Abdul from reaching down to detonate it, which the terrorist was attempting to do at this very moment. At the last second, Steve's body slammed into Abdul as the terrorist was grabbed and restrained from behind by terrified bystanders. Steve managed to knock Abdul off balance as he carefully grabbed the bomb and pulled it away from Abdul's reaching grasp. Abdul could not quite reach it and detonate it as he was overpowered and pinned by a hostile mob of people. Meanwhile, Steve positioned his body over the bomb to protect it from being accidentally detonated by some fool spectator knocking it, and he quickly figured to turn off the detonator switch to render it harmless. This he carefully did, breathing a big sigh of relief over what was just the scariest moment of his rough and dangerous life.

The police were soon on the scene, and detained Abdul, confiscated the bomb, and were intently questioning Steve in addition to other witnesses. Meanwhile, the general crowd within Times Square remained calm simply because they were unaware of what happened. The attempted bombing was viewed by most people, including the televised celebrity hosts, as just another fight that broke out in the crowd. In the excitement of the midnight celebration, nobody except in the immediate vicinity took any interest in it. Even the television cameras did not zero in on the action like they probably would have a couple of hours ago, when things were calmer and the commentators were desperately looking for anything to gossip about to pass time.

Rumors did initially go through the crowd from the place of confrontation, about some type of bomb present. But, within minutes this one rumor had become misinterpreted into ten different ones, some of them so ridiculous that most persons interpreted them as a hoax and simply laughed. Fortunately, no mass panic set in, so there was no stampede of people to escape that could easily turn into a riot. The police managed to keep things under control, and quietly took Abdul, the bomb, and witnesses away to the nearest precinct station. By the time the press hounds began hearing rumors and sensing a sensational story; Times Square was rapidly clearing of people and those involved in the incident had disappeared.

Once at the nearest police station, Abdul was booked on charges of attempting to commit a terrorist act, and the bomb was locked away as evidence. Steve and the other witnesses were questioned for part of the night, and once the cops were satisfied with their stories, released everyone with notice that they would be called to appear at a future court trial.

The next day, the Mayor of New York proudly announced on television in front of the press that the city's police department had bravely foiled an attempt of terrorism at Times Square the previous evening. He also added that a brave citizen had acted initially to alert the police, which probably prevented the terrorist act from succeeding. The press immediately went wild and began bombarding the mayor with questions. The mayor gave vague and sketchy answers, and soon cleverly gave the podium to the city's chief of police, to let him handle the press about more details.

Within days, most of the complete story of the incident was released to the press for printing. Despite the public being stunned and made a bit nervous about the threat of terror, the public's opinion of the city government and its police department was full of confidence. Especially, after the mayor announced that with the cooperation of the Federal Government and President, security in New York City and the United States would be considerably strengthened to prevent any future terrorists' attacks from ever being organized or conducted again within America. For now, Planet Earth was clearly shown that the United States had decisively won the opening round in the war against global terrorism!

As for Abdul the Camel and Steve the Pickpocket, the results of this incident changed both their lives forever. Steve became an instant national hero for his brave actions in foiling the terrorist plot. He very cleverly used this to his advantage, to change his life from a petty criminal to that of a successful respected citizen. Steve requested to the Mayor of New York, that as a reward for his heroism, the criminal charges on record for him be erased to a clean slate with the city's police department. The mayor gladly co—operated, and the justice system complied with Steve's request upon the mayor strongly hinting to Steve that he go straight from now on, and not screw up again.

Steve smartly decided to comply with the mayor's warning, and cleverly spent the next few months writing an autobiography about his criminal life as a pickpocket, and a detailed account about the night he stopped Abdul from blowing his terrorist bomb. The book was instantly a best seller on the New York Times list, and he now had enough money from the book's profits to make a comfortable living. Steve then took his income, and moved to a place where he would live his paradise dream! This place was the gambling mecca of the East Coast of America, none other than Atlantic City.

Steve with his money and notoriety, soon found himself hired as manager of one of the prominent casinos in that city. He would now spend the rest of his life, as a high—roller enjoying the pleasures of gambling, easy sexy women, and constant parties. The low—life pick—pocket from New York City, had now become the high-life roller of Atlantic City!

As for Abdul, he was eventually put on trial by the State of New York in a courtroom at Albany, New York. This was done because trying him in New York City would be too controversial and dangerous, owing to the extreme outrage and hate the public held for him there because of his attempted heinous crime. Owing to the overwhelming evidence against him, Abdul was quickly found guilty of attempted terrorism and sentenced to twenty—five years in prison, with possible parole at fifteen years with good behavior. There was some public outrage that this sentence was too light, and he should be given life imprisonment. The judge explained to his angry critics that because of Abdul's age, and the fact that he did not hurt anyone because the bomb never detonated, the set punishment was just. Since Abdul would be eighty years old at the earliest before he could ever be released from jail, what more harm could he be to society.

Abdul was then sent to prison in California for his own safety, amidst fears he might be killed while incarcerated in New York because of his infamous notoriety. He was placed in solitary confinement at San Quentin Prison near San Francisco. One of his close neighbors, would be none other than the infamous Charles Manson. Upon hearing the news that the Muslim terrorist would be a prison—mate, Charles had stated to show his powers of mind control on other inmates; that he would convert this nasty Muslim to his right-wing Neo—Nazi Politics. That would show the Muslim world, the power of Charles Manson! Charles additionally stated, that if he could not convert Abdul, well, he just might mess him up good. Abdul took the reports calmly, and decided that whatever happened, would be the will of Allah.

Surprisingly, Abdul was never physically accosted or converted to Fascism by Manson in the beginning of his sentence. In fact, Abdul immediately became a model prisoner. Abdul never caused any trouble, as he spent most of his time studying religion and quietly reading the Koran and Torah. At some point after a few years, Abdul decided to reform his life and atone for his sins. He decided to create his own religion in prison, that would be based on peace and non – violence.

The new religion's name would be, "Sunni – Shyster – Shiites." Abdul would ingeniously combine the best aspects of Islam with Judaism, to spread the word of justice and peace for all of mankind, Muslim and non – Muslim alike. Maybe this way, he could help to bring peace and prosperity to the world.

At first, everybody in prison and the press laughed at Abdul the Shyster. The laughing stopped however; when after five years in prison, he accomplished the impossible deed. This was that he miraculously managed to convert Charles Manson to his new – found religion! This conversion absolutely shocked the prison population, Manson's former followers, prison authorities, and the press. The shock became even greater when Charles instantly became a model prisoner, and spread Abdul's word as his main disciple. Manson was now a guy who treated and loved everybody with respect and compassion.

This amazing transformation, and the influence of Manson's new-found positive mind power, soon caused almost the whole inmate population of San Quentin to convert to the Sunni-Shyster – Shiites' movement. Much to the shock of the warden, the prison was soon a tranquil peaceful place where problems and violence hardly ever occurred. Ninety – percent of the inmates were now model prisoners! The prison became so amazingly peaceful with content prisoners, that justice systems worldwide were instantly studying San Quentin to see what could be learned to incorporate into their own prison systems.

By the tenth year of Abdul's confinement, his work and dedication in prison with the Sunni – Shyster – Shiites' movement was so successful, the governor of New York ordered the parole of Abdul on the recommendation of the California Governor. He was released with much controversy, nevertheless, quelled his critics quickly as he continued his great deeds by taking his new religion to the outside world. He then spent the rest of his life gaining massive converts from all other world religions, and the Sunni-Shyster-Shiites became a very powerful and wealthy movement. Abdul the Shyster used this wealth and power to finally help bring everlasting peace to a troubled human race in the twenty – first century.

The imperfect terrorist, had now become the perfect peacemaker!

War is not evil, nor is it hell, nor murder.  In fact, it is adventurous fun!
However, one thing is absolutely certain-FOR WAR IS SILLY!!

SGT. CURLY BUSCH-2104

War Formula: Politics=Power=No Common Sense-It is proven in history that war is the instrument of that power. Therefore: No Common Sense=War-The answer is: WAR IS SILLY!

SGT. CURLY BUSCH-2105

If everybody in the world realized that war is silly, then there would never be wars!

SGT. CURLY BUSCH-2106

The Literary Buccaneer was a true danger and menace to society! This Public Enemy #1, should have been hunted down and blown from the waters by the Royal Navies of America and Great Britain. It was an impossible task though, since this writer was a formidable two-edged sword-some sort of cross between Mark Twain and Karl Marx. A powerful combination indeed, striking terror in the establishment!

SGT. CURLY BUSCH-2108

## LE GRANDE FINALE-QUOTES!

A people who have been brought up on victories often do not know how to accept defeat!

NAPOLEON BONAPARTE-1813

**The revolution is over.  I am the revolution!**

NAPOLEON BONAPARTE-1800

## PROPOGANDA POSTER!

Bloody Field Marshal Von Busch sends out his patriotic message to the
youth of America.  The message is for them to join the new U.S. Army of the 22$^{nd}$

Century, in order to win the crusade against world evil, by waging the War of Horror! (see back cover)

The only known existing photograph of General George Hannibal Busch,

**(University of Texas Archives-2500 A.D.)**